Thomas Hardy

Thomas Hardy

Imagining Imagination
Hardy's Poetry and Fiction

BARBARA HARDY

THE ATHLONE PRESS
LONDON AND NEW BRUNSWICK, NJ

First published in 2000 by
THE ATHLONE PRESS
1 Park Drive, London NW11 7SG
and New Brunswick, New Jersey

Barbara Hardy has asserted her right
under the Copyright, Designs and Patents Act,
1998, to be identified as the author of this work

British Library Cataloguing in Publication Data
*A catalogue record for this book is available
from the British Library*

ISBN 0 485 11543 3 HB
0 485 12153 0 PB

Library of Congress Cataloging-in-Publication Data
Hardy, Barbara Nathan
Thomas Hardy : imagining imagination : Hardy's poetry and fiction / Barbara Hardy.
p. cm.
Includes bibliographical references and index.
ISBN 0–485–11543–3 (alk. paper) –– ISBN 0–485–12153–0 (pbk. : alk. paper)
1. Hardy, Thomas, 1840–1928 –– Criticism and interpretation. 2. Imagination in
literature. 3. Imagination. I. Title.
PR4757.I4 H37 2000
823′.8 –– dc21   99–054615

Distributed in The United States, Canada and South America by
Transaction Publishers
390 Campus Drive
Somerset, New Jersey 08873

Typeset by ensystems, Saffron Walden, Essex
Printed and bound in Great Britain by
The Athenaeum Press Ltd, Gateshead

For Sam Hynes

Contents

Acknowledgements   viii

References   ix

Introduction   1

1. Portraits of the Artist in the Novels   5
2. Centres of Creativity in the Novels   33
3. Good Times in *Jude the Obscure*:
   Constructing Fictions   57
4. Portraits of the Artist in the Poems   83
5. Arts of Conversation   106
6. The Poetry of Place   138
7. Sexual Imagination: the Monologues   160
8. Thresholds and Limits   179
   Inside and Outside   179
   Human Beings and Others   193
   The Supernatural   202
   Reticence   209

Notes   218

Select Booklist   226

Index   223

Acknowledgements

I am indebted to the following friends and colleagues: Michael Baron, Jerome Beaty, Jean Brooks, Richard Ellmann, Pat Fowles, James Gibson, Beryl Gray, Ian Gregor, Samuel Hynes, Kenneth Marsden, Toru Sasaki, Brian Southam and many Birkbeck students; also to the University of London Library, Birkbeck College Library, and the Chelsea and Kensington Libraries in the Old Brompton Road and Hornton Street. I have warm memories of visits to Ankara, Dorchester and Jerusalem, where I gave papers and enjoyed discussions on Hardy.

Chapters One, Two and Four are revised and extended versions of lectures originally given at the middle East Technical University at Ankara, for a seminar in memory of Dr Evin Noyan; Chapter One also draws briefly on my introduction to the New Wessex edition of *A Laodicean*; Chapter Three is a revision of a paper given at the Hebrew University of Jerusalem, published in *Rereading Texts/Rethinking Critical presuppositions. Essays in Honour of H.M. Daleski*, ed. Shlomith Rimmon-Kenan, Leone Toker and Shuli Barzilai, Frankfurt-am-Main: Peter Lang, 1997; Chapter Five and Six are based on lectures for the Hardy Society; and Chapter Eight is a revision of an essay in *Tensions and Transitions (1869–1990). For Ian Gregor*, ed. Michael Irwin, Mark Kinkead-Weekes and A. Robert Lee, London: Faber & Faber, 1990.

Discussions of Hardy from which this book has developed are in *The Appropriate Form (Athlone, 1971) Tellers and Listeners (Athlone, 1975), and Forms of Feeling in Victorian Fiction* (Peter Owen, 1985), but unlike my earlier writing this is about the poetry as well as the novels.

References

Quotations of novels are from the New Wessex Edition,
London: Macmillan, 1974–5, and quotations of poems
from *The Complete Poetical Works of Thomas Hardy*, ed.
Samuel Hynes, Oxford : Clarendon Press, 1984.

Introduction

The experience every artist shares and every artist treats is creativity. In nineteenth-century literature the subject was present but less central, conspicuous and self-conscious than it has become. Artistic self-concern is now a major, even a definitive, theme of postmodernisms, but there is a long line of European poems and novels concerned with art, as different from each other as Pope's 'Essay on Criticism' and 'The Dunciad' are from Verlaine's 'Art Poétique' or a Künstleroman like Goethe's *Wilhelm Meister* from Thackeray's *Pendennis* and Dickens's *David Copperfield*.

Arthur Pendennis and David appeared at almost exactly the same time, artist-heroes of novels in which the subject of art is subordinated to other themes. Thackeray and Dickens trace a novelist's inclination from childhood habit to adult success but the story of the career is reticent, the story of love and social experience stronger and more conspicuous. In other novels these authors motivate narrators who are not artists, like Barry Lyndon and Pip, tracing the acts of their imagination. George Eliot may present artists, Philip Wakem, for instance, or the Alcharisi, but they serve the story of Maggie Tulliver and Daniel Deronda; and only once, in the short tale *Mr. Gilfil's Love Story*, does she make an artist the central figure. Henry James writes about Roderick Hudson who is a sculptor, but more centrally and deeply about Rowland Mallett who is not: like Stephen Dedalus, Roderick is displaced as hero by an ordinary citizen.

As James develops Rowland, or Isabel Archer, Maggie

Verver and Strether, who are not narrators but what he called sensitive registers of experience, he is studying the cultural habitat, the manipulation of relationships, and the variations of viewpoint, problems for every human being but special problems for the artist. There are novels and poems of all periods in Western culture, in which the subject is not art but imagination, where the artist's life and mind is shown by refraction or indirection. Thomas Hardy writes novels in this tradition, in which his interest in art is indirectly presented in characters who are not artists. Like Jane Austen's and George Eliot's, his most interesting aesthetic introspections are oblique or sub-textual.

What are his special interests in imagination, as he writes novels about the imaginative life, in various forms? He is drawn to everyone's creativity, to the ordering and invention of our reveries, which look before and after in memory and anticipation, realistically and fantastically, and our social narratives of gossip, news, myths, lies and truths. Hardy knows as well as James that narrative imagination is partial and unreliable, but he shows this in his own way, not in the Jamesian drama of subjectivity but in his own rhetoric of provisionality.

We are given repeated reminders or warnings by his quietly omniscient narrators, or shown constructive acts in the minds and hearts of characters, which persuade us that the story only seems to be what is related. Hardy constantly insists that he is not to be taken literally but imaginatively, that his work records not beliefs and faiths but impressions and appearances. When he had second thoughts about his work, as he did in revising *Jude the Obscure*, whose downward turns and bleak ending made him anxious not to appear ideologically confident or systematically pessimistic, he altered small details of the text to make it more tentative. No doubt he was also motivated by a wish to correct the impression made by *Tess of the d'Urbervilles*, whose sporting President of the Immortals had been taken too literally. Everywhere we have the advantage of his scrupulous placings of imagination, more seems and seemings than in any other Victorian novelist, a rhetoric of admitted uncertainty which is congenial to the modern mind.

He is a great poet as well as a great novelist, and his two genres are closely interfused. Even though he was aware that you may get away with dogmatic opinion more easily in poems than in novels, the rhetoric of provisionality is present in his poems too, especially those in which he reaches out to comprehend otherness, in memories, ghosts, birds, beasts and flowers. Here too he gratifies our late twentieth-century critical interest in reflexivity. It is not my intention to emphasize the topicality of this self-reference. Though it has been claimed as a particularly modern concern, it is not. Everywhere in literature, from Homer onwards, literature is aware of itself.

In this book I have traced Hardy's imagining of imagination in novels and poems, through the minds of professional and unprofessional artists (architects, musicians and writers) though to a greater extent through the creativities like those in his elegies and nature poems, his rustic choruses, and his major characters from Gabriel Oak to Tess and Jude. I have also discussed particular forms and themes: acts and arts of conversation, the poetics of place, the sexual imagination, especially in the neglected narrative poems, and lastly, his concern, in prose fiction and poetry, with the thresholds and boundaries, verges and limits, which imagination is forced to meet and recognize, to cross or fail to cross.

In order to examine these indirections and sub-texts, I have looked closely and lengthily at individual passages, from time to time returning to the same text – even the same stanza or dialogue – to look at a new aspect, with the result of some overlap.

I am not trying to present the intrinsic, or the hitherto undiscovered, Thomas Hardy, but to emphasize one pre-occupation of a great artist who challenges our conception of the Victorian and the modern. The book concentrates on a single subject but I hope its close readings in his two main genres will show aspects of Hardy's radical, scrupulous and troubled imagination which I have not made explicit or central, and which are relevant to us as like him we turn from one century into another, understanding his ethics and politics better than many of his contemporaries could. Like him we hope for the best but take a good look at the worst, doubt but fight wars, hate nationalism but warm to regionalism, are anthropocentric but respect other lifeforms, cannot be optimists but try to be meliorists, criticize institutions but fail to improve them, accept history but hanker after freedom and the unconditional.

CHAPTER ONE

Portraits of the Artist in the Novels

Hardy was a novelist, short-story writer and poet, trained in architecture, liking to draw, brought up to play the violin, sing and dance. In his poem 'Rome: The Vatican: Sala Delle Muse' (1887)[1] he summons his composite Muse, 'an essence of all the Nine', to defend his artistic miscellaneousness and to emphasise the affective, intellectual and personal nature of his work. The worshipper of Form, Tune, Story, Dance and Hymn is reassured that his various genres are phases of one art, all aspects of the artist's thinking and feeling:

> 'I am projected from thee,
> One that out of thy brain and heart thou causest to be –
> Extern to thee nothing.'

Many of Hardy's characters, including his chief narrators in the novels, are portraits of the artist, but some are more creative than others, in ordering and unifying, in finding fresh language, in reaching out to the human and non-human phenomenal world. Some are professionally creative, some are noticeably but unprofessionally adept, particularly in narrative, some are what Henry James called sensitive registers of experience, not portraits of their author but images of inventive or empathetic genius.

Hardy's wisest imaginings of imagination are the least professional. They seem to be made at an intuitive as well as a conscious level of thought, and they are thoroughly individuated, made dramatic, generated in process and act. His explicit thoughts about art are interesting too, and some of his professional artists, whose art is often superficially or selectively characterized, are the occasion for fine comment, even if it is sometimes expressed in a laboured or matter-of-fact way.

In *Desperate Remedies*, Hardy's first novel (1871), for example, the introduction of the heroine's architect father Ambrose Graye, gives rise to undramatised and undemonstrated observations. Graye is said to have a 'sanguine receptivity' (prone to depression) and a 'quality of thought which, exercised on homeliness, was humour; on nature, picturesqueness; on abstractions, poetry. Being, as a rule, broadcast, it was all three' (Chap. 1). These are not commonplace comments, and their suggestiveness invites contemplation, but is not developed. Hardy rapidly sketches an artistic imagination and its work, its potential and realized gifts, but the gifts of Graye, a plot-precipitator but a background figure who is killed off in the first chapter, are in excess of the story's needs. Hardy has not yet learnt what to leave out, especially when tempted by self-reference, and this mind with 'broadcast' powers has no work to do in the novel. Graye's general susceptibility has, but that is not remarkable in one of Hardy's young lovers.

A more important character, Cytherea's lover Edward Springrove, poet and architect, is an obvious mouthpiece for Hardy's own poetic frustrations in the early days when he could not get his poems published and turned to the novel. Edward cynically says that poetry on emotional subjects is best given up, 'Poetical days are getting past with me, according to the usual rule', and concludes that successful architects need public not artistic skills, social energies not often combined with 'a fondness' for art. This too tells us something about the author but adds nothing to the novel. Springrove's expressive powers are not developed in the plot and relationships; Hardy is using the character indulgently and randomly.

One character in the same novel is more thoroughly, if not more convincingly, psychologized as an artist than these sketchy autobiographical figures – the illegitimate outsider Manston. Manston is a poet. His lyric 'Eunice', in the effusive style of Tennyson's 'Lilian', 'Isabel' and 'Margaret', though even slighter, is Hardy's first published poem, and he makes the most of it, printing it twice in the text and incorporating it as a major clue in the plot of crime and punishment. Named for Manston's wife, it uses – or abuses – the imagery of the composite Muse: impressionistic portrait, melody, transition and contour. The telltale image of blue eyes helps Springrove save his beloved from a bigamous consummation, in the nick of time:

> Eunice
> Whoso for hours or lengthy days
> Shall catch her aspect's changeful rays,
> Then turn away, can none recall
> Beyond a galaxy of all
>   In hazy portraiture;
> Lit by the light of azure eyes
> Like summer days by summer skies:
> Her sweet transitions seem to be
> A pinkly pictured melody,
>   And not a set contour. (Chap. 16)

More plausibly in character is Manston's music. He is like Mop Ollamoor in 'The Fiddler of the Reels', the musician in whose wild, 'lingual' and unorthodox fiddling, and the dizzy reels he commands, Hardy nervously and fascinatedly identifies the perils of wordless passion and riotous urge. Like Mop's demonic powers, Manston's sexuality is related to his performance as musician, and when he plays the organ in a storm he overwhelms Cytherea by notes which shake and bend 'her to themselves':

The power of the music did not show itself so much by
attracting her attention to the subject of the piece, as by
taking up and developing as its libretto the poem of her
own life and soul, shifting her deeds and intentions from
the hands of her judgment and holding them in its own.
(Chap. 8)

Powerful organ–music in a small room, exultant creative
glee, and the heroine's reluctant fascinated masochistic
submission, are not enough for the ambitious author, who
adds thunder, lightning[2] and hypnosis to the musical storm,
not to mention sensational personification. *Desperate Remedies* is overwritten in every possible way, as Hardy came
to realize – the master of understatement had a long way
to go. Like Iago, Manston is excessively motivated, and his
incredibly complicated attempts at seduction and bigamy
are not clarified by his artistic gifts. Still, Hardy is trying to
relate his character's sexual charm and power to creativity
and communication, and to make artistic energy and
imagination part of an affective whole. What is more, the
novelist who could play the fiddle and dance is recognizing
the danger of music, which Wagner knew was the brandy
of the damned.

The next two portraits of professional artists come after
his second novel, *Under the Greenwood Tree*, (1872) and do
something new in Hardy, in presenting women as professional artists. Elfride, the heroine of *A Pair of Blue Eyes*
(1873), writes and publishes a romantic novel, but she is
creatively unsuccessful compared with the men, the architect who is one of her lovers, the essayist and reviewer
who is another. Artistic careers help to spin the plot but
the artistic imagination has very little to do with the
relationships and passions. Elfride's novel is dismissed by
Knight, her critic and lover, as a weak historical romance,
and her authorship is pathetic though culturally plausible,
just right for her passive and constricted middle-class life as

a daughter of the vicarage with conventional ladylike 'accomplishments'. It plays a part in the novel, helping to direct the flow of reader's sympathy away from the conventional dominant male culture towards her victimized frailties. Her rather stupid clergyman father has a mechanically over-stressed habit – though it illustrates Hardy's narrative self-awareness – of starting to tell stories he cannot finish because they are 'too bad'. One of her lovers is an architect, but there is little about his work, and the other is an essayist and reviewer who – interestingly – writes in fragments and evades fiction. Her own writing, a romance based on Arthurian legend, and published under the male pseudonym, Ernest Field, like her talk, her loving and her dying, has probably more political significance than the author realized.[3]

The next novel, *The Hand of Ethelberta* (1876) is more consistently an artist-novel and more clearly feminist, but it is also more willed and mechanical, and much less passionately imaginative than *A Pair of Blue Eyes*. Unlike Elfride, Ethelberta is a heroine whose art is a central theme, discussed, developed and illustrated, though not adequately. In his biography *Young Thomas Hardy* Robert Gittings discusses several meanings of the key word 'Hand' but omits to mention the artist's hand. It is a versatile one: Ethelberta's is a composite Muse and she can put her hand to anything. Like her author, she first writes poetry, publishing the successful *Metres by E* (arch, but an improvement on the original intention, *Metres by Me*), but needs to support herself and better her family so moves on to more lucrative public story-telling.

Hardy gives 'two well-known lines' of her verse, quoted by one admirer in a 'slow soft' soliloquy as he gazes at her window, and overheard by another doing the same thing:

'Pale was the day and rayless, love,
    That had an eve so dim.' (Chap. 8)

Another poem, 'When tapers dim' is described as a popular choice for musical setting but we only get its title. Critical reception of her work includes some amused and highly emotional reponse, one generic preference, 'They are not quite *virginibus puerisque* . . . but I cannot help admiring her in the more reflective pieces; the songs I don't care for' (Chap. 9), and praise for sounding modest while handling 'curious subjects'. Her own judgement and imaginative self-awareness are suggested in a response to a setting of one song by Julian, her admirer, showing that she values intensity; and in conversation with her mother-in-law who criticizes a poem as 'ribald' but admits she doesn't know what the word means. Ethelberta – like her author, who often disclaimed autobiography – proposes the separation of life and art. Her writing is more 'ardent', 'gay and rapturous' than she is:

It would be difficult to show that just because I have written so-called gay and amatory verse, I feel amatory and gay. It is too often assumed that a person's fancy is a person's real mind. I believe that in the majority of cases one is fond of imagining the direct opposite of one's principles in sheer effort after something fresh and free; at any rate, some of the lightest of those rhymes were composed between the deepest fits of dismals I have ever known. (Chap. 10)

Ethelberta's articulation of Keats' negatively capable chameleon poet – or something like it – is at least unpretentious, but because her sentimental education and inner life are left untreated, once again we glimpse an artistic topic of importance to the author but not assimilated and dramatized. The novel succeeds where its predecessor failed, in putting the woman's career in the centre of the action and emphasizing it as a theme, and fails where it succeeded, in not suggesting the emotional life, as if Hardy were over-correcting the defect of *A Pair of Blue Eyes*.

Resembling her author in poetic range – reflective, pathetic and light – Ethelberta is like him in moving from lyric poetry to prose narrative. Her money-making narrative genre is not novel writing but the unusual profession of public improvization, an art which lets Hardy revise and represent his own, though not in fine detail. Once more we are told more than we are shown. In a nice stroke her less educated brother, who knows good narrative when he hears it, praises her for being able to tell a gripping story about anything at all, for instance about going from one room to another, a compliment echoing Wordsworth's insistence in 'Simon Lee, the Old Huntsman' that the good reader can find a tale 'in anything', though without its ethical implication. Unfortunately, Ethelberta's powers, unlike those of Wordsworth's narrators, are not shown in action.

The final twist of the story about storytelling, when she switches her genre from fiction to confessional autobiography, is a farewell performance which joins life and art: she takes the stage at a fashionable house-party to reveal her secret, the secret of her class. It is a good idea and potentially a good climax but left unperformed. If we think of his gifted amateurs it is clear that Hardy, like Wordsworth's minimalist narrator and gentle reader, can make a story out of anything, however small and ordinary, but the great narrator of everyday stories fails in this instance where a taste of oral story-telling is needed.

It is as if he cannot turn into monologue, in this story of improvised professional speech, what he grasps and renders so vividly and variously in the rustic monologue. It is a strange kind of literalist failure. His idea – the fascinating idea of turning from fiction to memoir and trying to make art from present-tense reality, – remains an abstraction. (The problem of narrating the intransigeant here-and-now was to tease Hardy's admirer Virginia Woolf, as we see at the end of *Orlando* and *To the Lighthouse*.) Hardy maddeningly summarizes what should have been acted out as dénouement, dulling what might have been an exciting open ending. His evolution of the stages in Ethelberta's career theoretically relates fiction to art and art to fiction but the relationship is never made performative. Ethelberta's narrative, like her poetry, is uncharacterized and unparticularized. Like his other formal *Künstlerroman*, *The Well-Beloved*, the novel's art fails to show an artist.

The next novel, *A Laodicean* (1888) has another professionally autobiographical character, George Somerset, a working architect and failed poet, but his real role and importance is that of the young romantic hero, loved, misunderstood and eventually rewarded. However, in his character and experience, the creative imagination is more successfully interiorized than in the previous novels, and Hardy does rather better in making ideas about art dramatic and individual. Somerset's 'modern' gift of 'unlimited appreciativeness' (not unlike Daniel Deronda's excessive empathy) is not left as an idea but given a psychic dimension. His sensibility and senses are animated in intense lyrical moments with Paula. Unlike Edward Springrove, Manston, Elfride and Ethelberta, he is given some interior life, and endowed with an emotional memory. For instance, he is shown returning to an old landscape of love, nervously and consciously stirred by his unexpected, and unexpectedly powerful, response. Hardy is learning to particularize the sentimental history, to dramatize his characters' affective life, and strong emotional incidents give some vividness and credence to the action as an artist's story. There are not many such episodes: Somerset's psyche is subordinated, made instrumental in the story of knowledge and power, in this case the woman's story.

Loss and gain are mixed. Paula Power is one of Hardy's most overtly feminist portraits, as her name suggests. More consistently and fully characterized than Ethelberta, she has some power because she is rich but weakened and frustrated because she can only act through men. Enterprising in architectural plans and high technology – she installs the electric telegraph – she does not attempt original art, and her blueprints of an ideal modernized castle are amateurish. But novels draw on the life of their authors in many ways, and beneath the surface of this novel, which is most obviously autobiographical in the hero's architecture, lie deeper affinities and motives.

Havelock Ellis reviewed the novel in the *Westminster Review* (1883), looking beyond the so-called rambling Victorian three-decker with its multiple plots and lack of conspicuous craft, which as a contemporary critic he underrated as a loose baggy monster. He was complimentary, judging Hardy's new novel to be 'perhaps more faultless, and certainly less mannered, than anything he had yet produced,' and praising its 'single thread of love-story' and 'exquisite workmanship', but his interest in form went beyond a concern for unity and elegance and his most original perception was a distinction between Hardy's method and that of 'many distinguished novelists, in which women are considered as moral forces, centripetal tendencies providentially adapted to balance the centrifugal tendencies of men'. He sees the novel's theme of intellectual, moral and psychological lukewarmth, or laodiceanism, embodied in the heroine's detachment, in which he spots her author's:

When Somerset asks Paula about her creed, she replies: – 'What I really am, so far as I know, is one of that body to whom lukewarmth is not an accident but a provisional necessity, until they see a little more clearly.' And this attitude of Paula's is one which we recognise as implicit throughout Mr Hardy's novels. Any more definite standpoint is nowhere plain.

What Ellis identifies in the novels before 1883 is a characteristic not only of Hardy's agnosticism and intellectual detachment, but of his artistic temperament too. It is like Keats' idea of negative capability, and important because it relates not only to the hero, the poet and architect to whose education and work have range and substance, but also to the heroine and her philosophy – or pseudo-philosophy, since Paula's mind is untrained and she is ironically named.

D. H. Lawrence once suggested that women – unfortunately distinguished from artists, at least for the purpose of this analogy – were 'like artists' in their fluidity, their refusal to take a shape, stay with it and rest content. Hardy also saw women as fluid, and this novel is about a man who is an artist and a woman who is only able to be one vicariously. Her laodiceanism is the equivalent of Somerset's artistic eclecticism, but they are not exactly the same thing. Laodiceanism involves uncertainty, eclecticism is grounded in choice. Laodiceanism hesitates between styles, eclecticism combines them. One is right for the uneducated woman, whose religious culture allows her to give a name to it, the other for the educated man. Laodiceanism is as close as Paula can get to negative capability, with its creative and intellectual advantages.

Whichever came first, concept or character, the idea had feminist implications. Paula has her chapel culture, and a smattering of literature and history, but little more. She calls herself a Hellenist, and has her own ideas about eclectic restoration of her castle, but cannot tell a trained architect from an ignorant dishonest builder. She can only be called educated, as she is, because women's education was superficial and patchy, as early feminists often complained. Careerless, women were trained for courtship and marriage, to be at worst a bore or irritant, at best a stay or stimulant. Paula's lack of education is thrown into high relief because of her position and money, and demonstrated in her relations with the men around her. She is an easy prey, both to the predatory men and to her own caprice and ignorance. Like the heroine of Hardy's first and unpublished novel *The Poor Man and the Lady*, she reflects his experience of being attracted by a woman of superior class as well as his notion of a modern – not yet quite a New – woman. In this novel she is an essential aspect of Hardy's attempt as the portrait of an artist.

His last artist-novel is *The Well-Beloved*, published in volume form after *Jude the Obscure* but written before it. In conception it is the most concentrated and ambitious of his novels about a professional artist's career and imagination, though as usual he links the specialized story of art with a love story. He does so more originally and integrally than in the early novels, where the young romantic hero's poetry and architecture have little to do with his emotions. Jocelyn Pierce's Platonic pursuit of the ideal is relevant both to his art and his loves, as well as having an autobiographical foundation. Hardy is dignifying his own emotional mobility while trying to analyse it, but the action of the ambitious love-story is mechanical, abstract, even ludicrous as Jocelyn shifts his attentions down the generations, honouring them in the name of the ideal. But what he is after is not necessarily silly or self-indulgent. Marcel Proust's Marcel is movingly and searchingly both lover and novelist, using creative memory to nourish passion, re-order experience, understand his sentimental history and justify the assays of narrative. In James Joyce's Stephen Dedalus sexuality is associated with the liberated imagination, freed from the demands, forms and restraints of religion, family and nation. Stephen's aphrodisiac vision of the wading girl, echoing Venus's appearance to Aeneas,[4] combines an erotically specific symbol with a professional decision and dedication.

Once again Hardy fails to fuse concept and art, and another insight is left as an abstraction. True, now he is writing an allegorical novel, for the only time, but the admission of fantasy in an obviously stylized and self-conscious genre does not make the artist-hero and his impossible object of desire either lucid or plausible. There is an intellectual link beween love and art: Pierston is said to use rejected and once-adored life-forms for his sculpture, and to embody desire in plastic forms, but there is no embodied connection between the sex and the sculpture. The elusive ideals in art and life stay separate; the twin subjects fail to reinforce each other causally, metaphorically or metonymically.

Representing the personal experience of art in art is – or should be, if pondered not merely mimicked – a problem for the artist, a special form of choosing to follow or avoid the life-story. The most interesting portraits of the artist combine the representation of art with the representation of life outside art, avoiding the narrowly professional image. Art is not enough of a subject, though imagination is. In the novel, Richardson cleverly used skilled, or sometimes significantly unskilled, amateur narrators: leading letter-writers like Pamela, Clarissa, Anna Howe, Harriet Byron and minor aspirants. George Eliot avoided the extraordinary artist's life, except on the periphery of her story, and a few of her poems. Their authors managed cleverly with David Copperfield and Arthur Pendennis the novelists and Clive Newcome the graphic artist, making them primarily active in what Coleridge calls the highroad of human life. Proust assimilated the analysis of a novelist's powers to the psychopathology of everyone's memory. In *Doctor Faustus* Thomas Mann made Adrian Leverkühn a musician, to write a specialized study of the dangers and destructiveness of imagination. Joyce needed the amateur artist, Bloom, to complement the poet-and-novelist, shown before his art matured. Hardy never attempts any of these imaginative compromises, and never successfully shows the professional artist.

With the singular exception of *Under the Greenwood Tree* (1872), a story about village music and musicians. Its music is quieter than in its predecessor, *Desperate Remedies*, like its style and narratives. This perfect novel concentrates on a low-life society and characters, and shaping and expressing them with a grace and cultural knowledge which show up the crudeness of the other earlier novels. Its artistic themes are entirely assimilated to character and plot. Hardy has moved from a novel containing professional artists treated superficially or melodramatically, to write about the music and musicianship he knew well. He shows it as part of the creativity of rural culture, steadily going about its quotidian business. A novel about music presenting an episode in the history of popular culture – the communality and disappearance of the church band and choir – it diffuses its themes of art comically and reverently, to remember and reshape a creative community. Imagination is everywhere, professionally in music, and in the informal, everyday narrative arts of gossip and reminiscence.

The original title was *The Mellstock Quire*. The novel is a love story as well as a story about the choir and band, and perhaps Hardy changed the title because it laid too much stress on music. The revised title from the song of that name in *As You Like It*, combines music, pastoral, and romantic comedy, and the sub-title is 'A Rural Painting of the Dutch School'. It is a deeply humane novel with a light touch, engagingly refusing to take itself too seriously, early work but assured and mature. The schoolmistress and organist, Fancy Day, 'the village sharpener' whose name airily suggests love and imagination, is witty, musical and articulate, but though her organ-playing supplants the music of the men her musical talent is not specified like theirs. They are choric, in singing and playing and experienced commentary on love, but they speak and perform too wittily and inventively to be a mere chorus. They are never patronized, never lumped together and never secondary.

Hardy has moved to an extreme in dramatic art. There is no generalization or analysis. Everything is performed, in action, conversation and animated narratives. But Hardy, fiddler, dancer, singer and listener, never forgets music. That story begins, as it ends, with natural music. The sounds of the winter trees are discriminated and orchestrated before the human voice is raised, also discriminated and joined in the Christmas carols. In Chapter Four the choir reminisces about the music of the past, threatened by modern innovations, harmonium and barrel-organ; and the conversation shows how naturally and unaffectedly the individual and collective life – for many levels and trades – was saturated in music. Music is shown at every turn, embedded in the culture. It is celebrated by racy, irreverent and generous story-telling, knowledge, judgement, professional discrimination, a tough-minded sense of history, and – above all – a sensuous appreciation of what the choir call their 'divine' art: they recall 'a serpent was a good old note: a deep rich note was the serpent' and admire 'the sweetness of the man of strings' (Chap. 4). Musical composition, instrumental music and song are praised in fluent long set-piece narratives and conversations which are images and proofs of prowess, pride and pleasure, characterizing the ensemble's parts, technique and direction in a wonderfully comic medium:

> Directly music was the theme old William ever and instinctively came to the front.
> 'Now mind, neighbours,' he said ... 'You two

counter-boys, keep your ears open to Michael's finger-
ing, and don't ye go straying into the treble part along
o' Dick and his set . . . and mind this especially when
we be in "Arise, and hail". Billy Chimlen, don't
you sing quite so raving mad as you fain would . . .'
(Chap. 4)

Hardy's delight in his choir and their music, with deep
personal roots in family memory, spills over in a number
of poems in which the performance continues, like the
wonderful 'Dead Quire' which revives the Mellstock
choir to follow 'viewless' the old route of the novel and
incorporates snatches of hymns in its hymn-form. These
poems, like others which overflow from *The Woodlanders*,
Tess of the d'Urbervilles, and *Jude the Obscure*, show the
interfusion of his two chief genres, and also display the
musical sensibility and knowledge which do not show so
intensely and concentratedly in the less musical and sensuous form of prose fiction but on which the novel's
density and depth depend. Tranter Dewy refers to the
rustic musician as 'an artist' and he knows what he is
talking about.

Hardy's skilful, humorous and benign tellers and listeners can be seen as portraits of their novelist in narrative
power and aplomb, but *Under the Greenwood Tree* is a
novel where creative imagination finds various forms,
implicitly embodied. To call it a reflexive novel – as it is,
profoundly – seems heavy-handed. Everyone is imagined
as imaginative: the child wondering what it is like inside
the cider-barrel, the keeper who keeps a double set of
furniture in anticipation of his daughter's wedding, love-
sick Dick Dewy seeing everything in love similes, Mrs
Penny remembering her dreams of a tall lover, Fancy Day
toying with visions of a grander marriage.

Of course the main imaginative energy is narrative.
The narrative chorus is the choir shifted to another genre.

One of the comments on narrative in the novels is the intelligent tranter's bland response to his wife's condemnation of Michael's story of chewing in six–eight time as coarse. His theory of narrative is funny and serious, not perverse, naïve or ridiculous:

> 'Well, now,' said Reuben, with decisive earnestness, 'that coarseness that's so upsetting to Ann's feelings is to my mind a recommendation; for it do always prove a story to be true. And for the same reason, I like a story with a bad moral. My sonnies, all true stories have a coarse touch or a bad moral, depend upon't. If the story-tellers could ha' got decency and good morals from true stories, who'd ha' troubled to invent parables?' (Chap. 8)

The novel is a collective, natural-seeming and virtuoso display of narrative performance in a variety of moods and modes. Some narratives are fired by a kind of detached zealous praise and generosity, like the tranter's reminiscences of Sam Lawson – 'good, but not religious good' – , others more simply self-engrossed in motive and theme, like Mrs Penny's deliciously tactless tale of her midsummer love-vision, her husband's tales of his shoemaker trade, and Michael Mail's story of musical eating. The last long and formal inset narrative, Thomas Leaf's shapeless wedding story under the greenwood tree, about the man who made money, is as deeply delicate and well-wishing as it is superficially maladroit.

The last story is a secret, not told. Fancy answers evasively as Dick looks forward to the complete truth-telling of married bliss, consciously reserving the 'secret she would never tell', in the last words. The novel silences the falsities of human utterance, to end as it began, with the unequivocal music of the green wood, this time not the sounds of leaves and branches but a bird, 'Hark! 'Tis the nightingale!'. In keeping with the book's temper, the heroine is not rapturous. Like its source-book *As You Like It*, the novel knows the real pastoral world too well to romanticize it, and this most assimilated of Hardy's literary sources is there in the background of the love story. It is in the title and in the unquoted bits of song, reminding us that 'most friendship is feigning, most loving mere folly' but never saying so. Best of all, the song with which Fancy shares the last lines is more daring than T. S. Eliot's nightingale song in *The Waste Land*, and more inter-textual. Its hybrid voice is unlike anything in Victorian literature, amazing but as far as I know unnoticed. Hardy's nightingale quotes Shakespeare, master of words, modulating from wordless music to a refrain of the song which gave its title to the novel and this final chapter:[5]

> From a neighbouring thicket was suddenly heard to issue in a loud, musical, and liquid voice –
> 'Tippiwit! swe-e-et! ki-ki-ki! Come hither, come hither, come hither!' (Part 5, Chap.2)

Hardy's presentation of the artist is at its best, as I said, when least specialized. The Mellstock band's collaborative art in *Under the Greenwood Tree* is the first sustained appearance, and model, for the rustic conversation which appears in all his novels, though occasionally diminished, as in *Jude*. It is Hardy's structural invention. There is nothing quite like it in earlier fiction except for the single scene at the Rainbow Inn in George Eliot's *Silas Marner*, and that is less a choric effort than a brilliant solo narrative from Macey the clerk as storyteller with encouraging response from the listeners. The only thing like it – and it is very like it – is I. Compton-Burnett's striking use of upstairs–downstairs' choruses.

Hardy makes his complex groups of not-so-simple narrators in a politically controversial way, using uneducated and sometimes naïve speakers. (For instance, Jan Coggan, Poorgrass and Pennyways in *Far from the Madding Crowd*. [1874]; Thomas Leaf; and Christian Cantle in *The Return of the Native* [1878].) Geoffrey Grigson[6] accused Hardy of creating and patronizing yokels, and a more recent and sympathetic critic, Paul Turner thinks the rustics dated and boring. These are unillustrated superficial readings. To read closely is to see Hardy's rural group-narrative as the opposite of condescending: its tellers and listeners are poets 'with a rough skin' as he called Farmer Springrove, intelligent, imaginative, sly, ironic, and liter-ary, drawing on the Bible, telling stories. Hardy's village simpletons are offensive to our modern sensibilities, but they are cared for in the community, given space and company in which they are creative too. The minor narrators are crucial in the interaction of fictional and actual history, creating and created by a rich felt life.

The gossip under the greenwood tree has no very bad news to tell; even the deaths are told with a light touch. In the tragic novels of course the gossips are messengers bearing good and bad news. In *The Return of the Native* Clym Yeobright is shocked and horrified by Susan Nun-such's superstitious attack on Eustachia, the news brought to him and his mother by successive articulate and breath-less messengers, in the manner of Greek drama and Shakespeare's *Macbeth*. Eustachia overhears people discuss-ing Clym's return, speculating and matchmaking, and announcing the welcome party at which the mummers perform. The chorus of gossips is made up of the furze-cutters and their hangers-on, always benign and some-times bumbling, like Shakespeare's comic magistrates and Watch in *Much Ado*. Hardy is like Shakespeare in making fun of his low-life choruses but honouring them too, bestowing on them eloquence, humour, wit and wisdom, the language of imagination. He mirrors the creative communication of the rural culture in which he grew up and at the same time constructs a micro-model of his novel.

This double action is striking in *Return of the Native* because there is a group leader, Timothy Fairway, who stands out more conspicuously than any of the expert narrators in *Under the Greenwood Tree*. The collective narrative and the individual genius are marked by energy, power and creative zest. Hardy's tellers are made in his own image, and reflect not only his narrative gusto but his inclination to celebratory, benevolent, venerating and often pessimistic narration. Hardy's lyrical homage to his paternal grandmother, Mary (Head) Hardy, in the poem 'One we knew' is an imaginative appreciation of memory, ordering, concentration, communication, creative delight, and a rhetoric which is skilful and spontaneous, crafty and impassioned. He praises her as an artist and a historian. Like Hardy himself.

Hardy is reconstructing and preserving a dying folk-art. Instead of collecting folk-tales and fairy-tales, as scholars do, he uses the novel for archeology and anthropology, as he looks at past and present by creating storytellers who look at past and present. The communal storytelling is less conspicuous than other rural arts and crafts, like the church music, the mummers' play, the Maypole ritual, Harvest festival and the Christmas dancing, because it is more integral and common. And also because it is still a part of live culture. Even in different times and circumstances, human beings are still story-telling animals. Story-telling was not an activity Hardy had to lament and memorialize. It was not disappearing or decaying.

Story-telling is an integral part of Hardy's own stories. His choric narratives are observed and constructed as people work, play, relax and keep tradition and history on the move. The placing of narrative and social conditions in context is faithful, lucid and functional, though so quiet and subtle as sometimes to pass unnoticed.

Hardy's imagining of the collective imagination presents the world of work, and its intermissions of leisure, and ritual celebratory time-marks. Function is also masked by individuality, as so often in Shakespeare. The analysis of folk-narrative is both end and means; and the social conditions of Wessex working-class life, reflected and invented, are understood and artistically constructed in ways which realize, motivate and thematize telling and listening.

Acts of telling are less clearly obviously or precisely related to rhythms of the body and the tools of the trades than work-songs associated with rowing and reaping and marching, but the association is there. Just as womens' hairdressers today have their conversational gambits, politely asking if the client is going somewhere special, so in *The Return of the Native* Timothy Fairway, all-round gifted craftsman, tells 'true stories' while cutting the villagers' hair (presumably free of charge) on Sunday mornings. The sawyers and trimmers in Melbury's timber yard in *The Woodlanders* talk while they work, with sufficient energy, breath and freedom to tell stories and listen. We are usually left to see the connection between work and narration, though Hardy's omniscient narrator sometimes draws our attention to the habit and the habitat:

> Copsework, as it was called, being an occupation which the secondary intelligence of the hands and arms could carry on without the sovereign attention of the head, allowed the minds of its professors to wander considerably from the objects before them; hence the tales, chronicles, and ramifications of family history which were recounted here were of a very exhaustive kind. (*The Woodlanders*, Chap.4).

Like his other rustic narratives from *Desperate Remedies* to *Tess*, the gossip in *The Return of the Native* is fully and

– it seems – effortlessly contextualized, in many ways. It is physically and socially facilitated by the habitual rhythmical labour of the turf-and-furze cutter, and the hangers-on who enlarge the novel's community. The gossip is consistently directed towards the main characters and their love stories, and the choric performance is crucial, with the question-and-answer about Wildeve and Thomasin, for example, and the anecdote of the forbidden banns – motivated with extreme naturalness since Timothy is an eye-witness, and the relaxed Humph, a less zealous church-goer, needs to be told. The furze-cutting, like the copsework, or cider-making in *Desperate Remedies*, gathers a crowd and gives leisure for telling.

When the work is too physically demanding the absence of narrative confirms Hardy's social experience and tact, as at the end of *The Return of the Native* when Timothy Fairway, the star storyteller, is hard at work on the making of a feather-bed, helped by the Cantles and Humphrey, friends we have seen and heard at gossip and reminiscence from the bonfire scene at the beginning to this last prelude to happy-ever-after marriage. It might be a final performance from a familiar ensemble whose work and talk began and punctuated the novel, a varying group but always with Timothy as lead, Humphrey as a laid-back, less brilliant but respectable second, Grandfer Cantle sporting the humours of old man and once-young blade, and the 'maphrotight' and simpleton Christian as foil and feed. As they benevolently toil over the home-made feather-bed, laboriously filling the mattress, and the air, with feathers, the conversation proceeds in fits and starts, with scarcely any narrative at all. The scene is nearly all action and object. Hardy's great narrative of making (like no-one's, except Lawrence's in *Sons and Lovers*) is so faithfully specific that his reader learns how to make a feather-bed too. For this chattering chorus it is the exception which proves the rule, a narrative minimalism where there has been profusion, because Hardy knows, though chooses not to say, this hard work would not leave breath for story-telling. His negative is as telling as his positive.

Timothy Fairway is the minor character who reminds us that in life there are no minor characters. As narrator-in-chief he tells many stories, but never his own. Like all artists, even those who try for impersonality, he is never quite impersonal. He is a natural leader, gossip and village historian, qualified by wit, humour and sensibility, and a modicum of tact. He is a good teller because he is highly sensitive and impressionable – he is deeply impressed by Mrs Yeobright's forbidding of the banns – but detached. Though he loves to take the floor, he can listen, and always knows whom he is talking to, with the exception of the only occasion when he is guilty of tactlessness, mentioning 'the man no woman at all would marry' in the company of Christian Cantle, whom the cap unfortunately fits.

He never tells his own story, but we piece together the ghost of an autobiographical subtext. He is cynical – or decidedly unromantic – about marriage, and in his writerly narrative we read between the lines and accumulate minute and apparently casual details, accreting bits of his story from stories about other people. His anecdote about seeing the mark of a previous groom when he is signing the register at his marriage, for instance, is a brief personal digression from the main stream of gossip:

'Couldst sign the book, no doubt,'said Fairway. 'if wast young enough to join hands with a woman again, like Wildeve and Mis'essTamsin, which is more than Humph there could do, for he follows his father in learning. Ah, Humph, well I can mind when I was married how I zid thy father's mark staring me in the face as I went to put down my name. He and your mother were the couple married just afore we were, and there stood thy father's cross with arms stretched out like a great banging scare-crow. What a terrible black cross that was – thy father's very likeness in en! To save my soul I couldn't help laughing when I zid en, though all the time I was as hot as dog-days, what with the marrying, and what with the woman a-hanging to me . . .' (Chap. 3)

Fairway's imagery is comically exaggerated, giving a taste of his quality, usually reserved for stories about other people, like his complimentary anecdote about Wildeve's supposed bride's father. On this occasion he is ably seconded by Sam and prompted by the Cantles and Humphrey, but he is the creative orator speaking an encomium for the gifted dead:

'. . . neighbour Yeobright, who had just warmed to his work, drove his bow into them strings that glorious grand that he e'en a'most saw'd the bass-viol into pieces. Every winder in church rattled as if it were a thunderstorm.' (Chap. 5)

His own story is more than marginalized, it is kept almost entirely out of sight. We get occasional references to his wife, and in another digression from the Yeobright story she is even quoted, in her slim and modest youth when she raced for a smock and brought news of Yeobright's collapse:

' "Well, whatever clothes I've won, white or figured, for eyes to see or eyes not to see" (a' could do a pretty stroke of modesty in those days) "I'd sooner have lost it than have seen what I have . . .".' (Chap. 5)

Timothy's jovial dance invitation to Susan Nunsuch, 'Susy . . . my honey', is accompanied by the mention,

serious or joking, of her husband – 'son of a witch' –
snapping her up her from him many summers ago. These
are snatches of personal narrative, dry or detached in tone,
never seriously emotional, nearly always subordinated to
another subject. We piece together passing comments and
digressions, like joining dots in a child's puzzle, but the
picture is never completed. Margin and text never quite
change places, Fairway stays in his place, the all-round
blunt humorous man, indulging the glimmer of a boast
about the moon not being new when he was born, a
leader in activities of work and leisure, never accompanied
by his wife, who is invariably absent, even in the one
scene in his own house, the making of the feather-bed.
On that occasion he remembers giving a feather-bed to
his own daughter, in the single mention of his issue.
Where is Mrs Fairway? She is not dead, because he refers
to her as if she is still alive, 'When I think what she'll say
to me now without a mossel of red in her face', but
unfortunately we never hear what she says now, she never
appears, is never mentioned by anyone except Timothy,
and at the bed-making it is Christian who helps him get
food and drink for the helpers.

   She is a beautifully absented character, and her witty,
enigmatic and intelligent husband is the subdued narrator,
the average sensual man. He is the settled native, at home
in the work, traditions and rituals of the heath, where he
plays his leading part. He balances Diggory Venn's more
sinister-seeming and isolated but more involved, benevo-
lence and power. He is the great story-teller whose own
life-story is withheld, but the withholding adds a dimension to his character as narrator and man, creates perspective for the novel's population, and blurs the edges of the
novel, like frame cutting through image in an impression-
ist painting. It is perhaps because *The Return of the Native*
involves a full show of the community in which to be
native is problematic and central, that Hardy constructs

such an intricate and consistent pattern of choric narration, with leader, hierarchy and coded subtext. In other
novels the narrative chorus is less differentiated, the cooperative work of several tellers, a crowd of talkative
humours, types of mind, character, status and trade. There
is a diffusion and variation of function, of course, and
different characters emerge and retreat to play their briefly
prominent parts, like Thomas Leaf telling his eager naïve
wedding-tale for his big moment before sinking 'into
nothingness again', or the elegiac Mother Cuxsom in *The
Mayor of Casterbridge*. Hardy's minor narrators bear the
imprint of their author as they praise and forgive the dead
and well-wish the faulty living, like Leaf offering his flat
story or imagining the life of his clever brother who died
when he was four hours and twenty minutes old. Hardy's
praise is not simple-minded; indeed, it is often ironic, like
the Mellstock quire's backhanded compliments to their
rude, neglectful and unspiritual vicar. His understatement
and slyness are seasonings which preserves the praise and
nostalgia from sentimentality and condescension.

Mother (or Mrs) Cuxsom is one of the exceptions, like
the postmistress Mrs Leat and Grandma Oliver, to Hardy's
preference for the predominantly male narrative chorus.
Women tend to participate in his social story-telling
briefly, as questioners providing a brief cue or comment,
like Olly Dowden and Susan Nunsuch, but with some
exceptions in special social situations. Mrs Cuxsom fulfils
the traditional gossip's or nurse's function – she has
ancestors in Shakespeare and Dickens – as she tells the
comic–pathetic story of Susan's death. The experienced
wise woman assisting at the mysteries of sickness and
death, and endowed like Fairway with a dialect and
rhetoric rooted in the rhythms, imagery and wisdom of
folk-narrative, she reminds us of Mistress Quickly narrating the death of Falstaff in *Henry V*. As we saw in Fairway,
Hardy likes to set narrative within narrative, and Mrs

Cuxsom quotes the direct speech of the dying woman, doubling and reinforcing the effects of a model funeral compliment, brilliantly particular, cleanly unsentimental, eloquently matter of fact:

'And she was as white as marble-stone,' said Mrs Cuxsom. 'And likewise such a thoughtful woman, too – ah, poor soul – that a' minded every little thing that wanted tending. "Yes," said she, "when I'm gone, and my last breath's blowed, look in the top drawer o' the chest in the back room by the window, and you'll find all my coffin clothes; a piece of flannel – that's to put under me, and the little piece is to put under my head; and my new stockings for my feet. . . . And there's four ounce pennies, the heaviest I could find, a-tied in bits of linen, for weights . . ."' (Chap. 18)

Her final words in this speech are truly conclusive as she records the dwindling of the personal life:

'. . . all her shining keys will be took from her, and her cupboards opened; and little things a' didn't wish seen, anybody will see; and her wishes and ways will all be as nothing.'

The small scale of the imagined losses is right for this obituary praise of such a passive existence. It is not wholly passive, however, and the valedictory words anticipate the telling of those deep secrets Susan Henchard did not wish to be known, which shaped destinies after her death.

Mrs Cuxsom's individually sympathetic renewal of old ritual is matched by Abel Whittle's sharp and spare praise after Henchard's death, in his comic–pathetic encomium. Abel is not such a vivid imagist or lyrical speaker as Mother Cuxsom but his praise has its own poetry, and it is rhetorically marked by repetition, dialect words like 'taties' and 'wambled', genuine-sounding unconscious humour, 'He was kind-like to mother when she wer here below, sending her the best ship-coal, and hardly any ashes from it at all . . .' with dignity of periphrasis, 'he's gone' and 'here below'. The merging of traditional forms with a literal and over-circumstantial narrative like that of garrulous Mistress Quickly and Mrs Nickleby, is right for the uneducated poor man of sensibility, another felt renewal.

No single narrator stands out in the talkative sawyers' yard of *The Woodlanders*, where storytelling is a generative collaboration. One after the other the men relate, reflect, add, question, prompt, agree, and of course, like any Greek chorus, inform the reader in wonderfully disguised exposition, with a touch of forecast, as they work and discuss their master's business, several generations uncovering layers of familiar history. As always, the rambling gossip and anecdote deepens our understanding:

Creedle said:
'He'll fret his gizzard green if he don't hear from that maid of his. Well, learning is better than houses and lands. But to keep a maid at school till she is taller out o' pattens than her mother was in 'em – 'Tis a tempting o' Providence.'
    'It seems no time at all since she was a little playward girl,' said young Timothy Tangs.
    'I can mind her mother,' said the hollow-turner. 'Always a teuny, delicate piece; her touch upon your hand was like the passing of wind . . .'.
    'Mr Winterborne's father walked with her at one time,' said old Timothy Tangs; 'but Mr Melbury won her. She was a child of a woman and would cry like rain if so be he huffed her. (Chap. 4)

Such telling does more than answer to the novel's title,
in communal energy, it also yields its own apt poetry in
figurations of nature, rough, 'fret his gizzard green', and
delicate, 'her touch . . . like the passing of wind' and 'cry
like rain'. Creative wisdom merges individual voices with
the ancient common language of proverb, old saw, and
bible.

Hardy takes his creative folk-gossip for granted, adding
little or no analysis or commentary, and it is more dialogic
– in every sense – and more original than the explicitly
discussed imagination of the artists proper. It is more
assimilated to the novel too, though it may have loose
ends or incomplete sub-texts reaching out imaginatively,
in Timothy Fairway's private life or Clym Yeobright's
career, disrupting neat unity and stretching measured span,
to question the limits of fiction.

CHAPTER TWO

Centres of Creativity in the Novels:
from Gabriel to Tess

Hardy's professional artists and his choruses perform in public, but the deepest and most complex centres of creativity in his novels are private and unperformed. There is little or no explicit comment on their powers, which are assimilated to the everyday acts of telling and speaking and projecting. Such characters are Gabriel Oak, Eustachia Vye, Marty South, Michael Henchard, Tess, Sue and Jude. They are not equally developed in creativity: some sustain or develop imaginative energy, some show it irregularly or rarely. Gabriel, Marty and Tess are capable of what Keats called the Shakespearean imagination, or negative capability, but the creativities of Eustachia and Henchard are ingrown and distorted versions of the egotistical sublime. Jude's creativity, and to some extent Sue's, is developed then slowly and surely destroyed. Like George Eliot, Proust and Joyce, perhaps more austerely, Hardy refuses to romanticize triumphs of imagination.

He seems to have found it liberating to create these powerful centres of creativity in characters who are not professional artists, perhaps to avoid his professional experience, perhaps to celebrate common creativity. He imagines imagination variously, in its originality, inventiveness, combinativeness, unselving and recreation of self. He endows characters with original language, for meditations and communications which are never explicated, framed or published as art. He does not romanticize creative simplicity or naïveté. Neither his rustic storytellers nor his heroes of creativity warble wild native woodnotes, but use imagination rationally as well as passionately, often judiciously and nearly always consciously.

Tess Durbeyfield is his best artist. She does not suddenly spring to life towards the end of Hardy's fiction writing but benefits from his experiments with earlier imaginative characters, to develop out of them. One of her most sensitive predecessors is Gabriel Oak, like Timothy Fairway a pastoral leader in his community but also a major character in the novel. In a modest way he is a musician, and his flute, like the Trumpet-Major's trumpet and Angel Clare's harp, is a sign and a metaphor. Hardy is preparing Tess's more sophisticated and analytic meditations on nature when he makes Gabriel show an imaginative response to the night, seeing the stars with a shepherd's eye but also in 'an appreciative spirit, as a work of art superlatively beautiful'. He is alert to beauty and to distinctiveness, and to his own position as observer. Seeing the stars when he is alone at night, in this same scene, involves an imaginative geographical obliteration of his surroundings, 'there seemed to be on the shaded hemisphere of the globe no sentient being save himself'. 'Seemed', of course, for the second time in the paragraph, and the typical wary surmise takes a further turn, 'he could fancy them all gone round to the sunny side' (Chap. 2). This psychic stirrring, these sharp personal moves of the mind followed step-by-step as they gather momentum, are just what is missing and needed in the professional portraits and what energizes the centres of consciousness and their novels.

These characters may be particularized, as Gabriel often is, in a free indirect style, or given an eloquent idiolect which draws on tradition and the individual talent. After Gabriel's flock is led to destruction by the young dog, Hardy registers the shepherd's intense grief and apprehen-

sion, in an objective correlative located in Gabriel's
imagination. As he recovers from the immediate shock
and stupor to say with generous love 'Thank God I am
not married' Hardy creates for him – and makes him
clearly recognize – an imaginative act which externalizes
his emotion and reinforces it:

> Oak raised his head, and wondering what he could do,
> listlessly surveyed the scene. By the outer margin of the
> pit was an oval pond, and over it hung the attenuated
> skeleton of a chrome-yellow moon, which had only a
> few days to last – the morning star dogging her on the
> left hand. The pool glittered like a dead man's eye, and
> as the world awoke a breeze blew, shaking and elon-
> gating the reflection of the moon without breaking it,
> and turning the image of the star to a phosphoric streak
> upon the water. All this Oak saw and remembered.
> (Chap. 5)

It is a curious passage, perhaps bearing the trace of
improvisation. Hardy presents the scene first as an omniscient author's description, then in the last sentence transforms it to reveal Oak's own imaginative figuration. The
process inclines the reader to re-read the conventional
direct style as the free indirect style in a shy or even
awkward form. Gabriel is not initially given the responsibility for the morbid metaphors of desolation but when
he is allowed to see, remember, and impress the natural
scene in a spontaneous act of symbol making, the transformation is made. In one imaginative stroke – or strictly
speaking, two – Hardy conveys Gabriel's capacity to feel,
contemplate, and generalize feeling.

His imagination is most active or shown most actively
in scenes of isolation like this, but his love speeches are
also balanced, as he says, 'between poetry and practicality'
like his night visions. He imagines married life in simple

diction but elegantly balanced clause structure, repetitions and effective synecdoche:

> 'And at home by the fire, whenever you look up, there I shall be – and whenever I look up, there will be you.' (Chap. 4)

Delightful to the lover, this lyrical imaging of domestic stability and warmth does not attract the beloved, whose distaste for the enclosed intimacy is unmistakable in her repudiating repetition, 'Why, he'd always be there, as you say; whenever I looked up, there he'd be': vision and revision are harshly written. When Gabriel makes his last loving declaration at the end of the chapter there is more repetition, ordered rhythm, increment and rise, the form and feeling of poetry

> 'I shall do one thing in my life – one thing certain – that is, love you, and long for you, and *keep wanting you* till I die'.

Gabriel's creative inner life is vividly and explicitly recorded in the narrative: he 'tenderly' regards Bathsheba's image 'beneath the screen of closed eyelids . . . busy with fancies, and full of movement, like a river flowing rapidly under its ice', and enjoys 'the pleasures of the imagination' (Chap. 8). At the end of the novel the colloquial poetry of his direct speech is used for the simple fine conclusion, so simple that we hardly notice the grace and balance which articulate the fond happy humour of rewarded love:

> 'I've danced at your skittish heels, my beautiful Bathsheba, for many a long mile, and many a long day; and it is hard to begrudge me this one visit.' (Chap. 56)

Eustachia Vye's first utterance is a sigh, long and impassioned, singling itself out from the whisper of Egdon's mummied harebells, the natural non-human sound which the narrator presents in a metaphorical and self-styled 'fetichistic' way. Our attention is drawn to imagination before Eustachia's passionate articulation is distinguished, in its egocentric fervent fantasies. Ignorantly and irrationally she reshapes her life, and other lives too, pressing the pattern of her wishes. Like Gabriel's her imagination is given its own poetry, a selfish poetry. Her imagination is precisely imagined, individuated in detail. It is contrasted, as Tess's will be, with the duller articulation and vision of educated orthodox men. She is a symbol-seer, appropriating the moon's eclipse, 'our time is slipping' (Bk 3, Chap. 4) but not a conscious and consistent analyst, and is amazed when Clym Yeobright reads 'friendliness and geniality' into the faces of hills. Her imagination is excited by hearing Clym's and other voices in talk, and Hardy describes it as movement, cyclical process, and a generated excitement. He imagines her awareness of imagination's frail, partial subjectivity:

'She glowed; remembering the mendacity of the imagination, she flagged; then she freshened; then she fired; then she cooled again. It was a cycle of aspects, produced by a cycle of visions'. (Bk 2, Chap. 3)

Intelligent enough to acknowledge imagination's unreliability, she still persists in shaping aspects and vision, telling a story about the future in a strong crude desire constructed by, and constructing, the stereotypes of her culture:

A young and clever man was coming into that lonely heath from, of all contrasting places in the world, Paris. It was like a man coming from heaven. (Bk 2, Chap. I)

This figuration in the free indirect style is crude, but the narrator's image of her creativity is sometimes more vivid and complex, suggesting positives and negatives. Hardy figures its rapture and dynamism – as he does in the brimming river of Gabriel Oak's visionary desire – but does not forget the self-centred and commonplace nature of its action, the context of a woman's blank life and need, in her class and community. When the author of Rosamond Vincy's fantasy life in *Middlemarch* drew attention to the dangerous emptiness of a woman's 'whole mind and day', she was clear about the relationship between that emptiness and the imaginative filling. Hardy also sees the contrast between the actual and the imagined habitat, but does not draw political conclusions about a woman's imagination:

> That five minutes of overhearing furnished Eustachia with visions enough to fill the whole blank afternoon. Such sudden alterations from mental vacuity do some-times occur this quietly. She could never have believed in the morning that her colourless inner world would before night become as animated as water under a microscope and that without the arrival of a single visitor. The words of Sam and Humphrey on the harmony between the unknown and herself had on her mind the effect of the invading Bard's prelude in 'The Castle of Indolence', at which myriads of imprisoned shapes arose where had previously appeared the stillness of a void.
>
> Involved in these imaginings she knew nothing of time. (Bk 2, Chap. 1)

Once more Hardy stays on the cautious narrator's side of the free indirect style: the generalization in the second sentence makes no gender distinction, and the scientific and literary figures for transformation may not derive

from Eustachia's experience. But the excited recognition
of creation is hers, 'She could never have believed . . . she
knew nothing of time'. Hardy is not always contemplating
the conditions of gender, and he sometimes seems
charmed by his heroine's creative transformations, which
he knows perfectly well are corrupt and destructive, in
contrast with Clym's benign and quietist vision. Eustachia's narrator is in danger of being carried away, as he
excitedly imagines her excited imagination.

Michael Henchard's is another dangerously unin-
structed and enclosed imagination. His imagination seizes
authority long before he takes office as Mayor of Casterbridge. His self-centredness, and also his social motives,
are made plain before he sells his wife Susan, so imaginatively and appallingly. Talking of marriage he says

'I did for myself . . .'

and

'if I were a free man again I'd be worth a thousand
pound before I'd done o't. But a fellow never knows
these little things till all chance of acting upon 'em is
past'. (Chap. I)

This is a lachrymose drunken grouse but it is also a
creative fiat. Henchard's 'If ' keeps company with Faust's
invocation of the devil, Alice's fantasy about looking-
glass, and Kafka's K's adoption of a Land Surveyor's job
in *The Castle*. Like Faust, Alice and K, Henchard makes a
fantastic hypothesis which becomes 'real', and like them
he is startled by his own imagination.

'If I were a free man again': it is the common fantasy
of freedom and the unconditional. His is not the only
fantasy which uses stimulants: Faustus does magic, Alice
falls asleep and dreams, Henchard gets drunk. In their

stories, the shift from subjective fantasy to objective event is helped by the abnormal or the pathological. Reality is given an extra tilt. Drink loosens Henchard's reason, and a wish is startlingly granted: his wife-auction finds a bidder and he is free to start again. Power is embodied in a suggestion of magic. Fantasy is made real in a politically visible context: marriage, poverty and rural unemployment, cheap drink, and women regarded as chattels. Social contexts are clear, but here is something dreamlike about the auction scene, something uncanny and creative, because of the brilliant articulation of Henchard's mad wish, because of the immediate answer, and because of the ritualistic nature of the challenge and the response.

The minute Henchard utters the wish for freedom the last bid is heard from the horse-auction, giving him his idea of a practical solution, and the auctioneer's last proposal is immediately accepted by a 'loud voice from the doorway'. It is a stranger's voice, like Fate, solicited – traditionally, devils and fairies need a human invitation – by a drunken dreamer who wakes from nightmares to find they are true and 'not dreams'.

Hardy conceives this tragic hero as an uneducated and superstitious man, whose first tragic act of imagination is followed by another, a ritualistic vow and contract to abstain from drink for ten years. Constructed by tragic history, in the novel and by the novel, Henchard uses imagination to behave as if he were free, hubristically, fantastically, and fatally taking a hand in his own destiny. His initiative is a destructive and imaginative act, as deeply irrational, visionary and tragic as the precipitating plan of King Lear. We should not be blinded by the obvious hateful fault of drunken wife-selling – a historical example but also a metonym – to the expansive radical desire for social freedom behind it.

There is little power of generalization shown in Henchard and little specific psychic detail – he is hardly ever made introspective. This does not matter. Like Gabriel Oak though with tragic profundities, Henchard is given his individual language of imagination. Words make him the most sensitive and aspiring character in the novel, the centre of disturbance, subversion, intensity and value. He places and outstrips the rational unimaginative survivor Farfrae as significantly, and as sympathetically, as Shakespeare's Antony and Cleopatra place and outstrip Octavius Caesar. Hardy, not Dickens or even George Eliot, is the nineteenth century's Shakespeare.

Like some of Shakespeare's characters, Henchard is at his most imaginative as he is imagined rising to the occasion of death. He keenly sums up his tragic experience, articulating the sense of self, almost generalizing. The expressive will pencilled on a crumpled scrap of paper is, like Timon's, made public by a humble man who cannot read. It is a testament of feeling, not a list of legacies, and its expression of its author's strong will unmakes the legal metaphor, presenting human will literally, freshly and profoundly. Like other acts of willing, it is well-meaning and sad, as it joins feeling for self and feeling for others, pride and humility, self-assertion and self-abnegation. Being Henchard's, and soberly composed, it admirably avoids self-pity and self-reproach. It is a formal and literate document: the unschooled man has been educated by office, and its two irregular spellings, 'flours' and 'murning', with the slightly awkward passive form, 'no-body is wished to see my dead body' are realistic, unemphatic, too dignified to be marked as error. The document is placed, in class, without condescension, like Mistress Quickly's obituary for Falstaff.

The first sentence shows a selfless priority: 'That Elizabeth-Jane Farfrae be not made to grieve for me' is sternly self-effacing but recognizes that she may grieve, as the impracticable extremity of the wish registers extravagant love and remorse. The will is piercingly pathetic, preserved from sentimentality by its particularized language and emotion. Its intense unselving recognition of other people, at the point of death, throws into relief the untragic and more commonplace survivals of Farfrae and Elizabeth-Jane. In form and feeling, this is tragic writing, about imagination.

The refusal of rites is ritualistic, and its listing and balanced ampersands are heartbreaking in solemnity, uttering isolation and loss as coolly as possible.[1] The wish that no man remember him makes an ironic but apt conclusion to the will, the life, and – almost – the tragic novel. It confirms his status as hero, like the book's title, which knows that not one of the novel's readers will ever think of Farfrae as the Mayor of Casterbridge, despite his office. The title is a knowing and subtle stroke of self-conscious art, an original way of saying that a loser in life may be a hero in art.

Elizabeth-Jane cries 'what bitterness is there!' but she knows less about her stepfather than the reader. There is bitterness but love and generosity too, an intensity of feeling which goes beyond self-indulgence, a proud self-humiliation which marks a kind of achievement. It finds a language which avoids self-pity, instead of claiming justice, pity or admiration like Cleopatra and Othello, who at the point of death step up their claims to be tragic and heroic. Henchard does the opposite.

His willed wish for no mourners or flowers is a negation of elegy, converted into a positive by the reader. Giles Winterborne's elegy in *The Woodlanders* is spoken by Marty, another imaginative character. Isolated, without a technical claim to be chief mourner, Marty renews the ancient vegetation ritual of health and faith, the funeral gifts of memorial, hope, praise, flowers and sympathetic magic. Hardy moves us by characters who are not excessively noble, like Henchard and Marty. Henchard is faulty in many ways, but the more virtuous Marty is jealously

delighted when her rival leaves her to hug her superior
fidelity and sole possession of Giles. Marty gathers up all
we have known of her, in mourning words which stay on
the human side of sublimity:

'Now, my own, own love,' she whispered. 'you are
mine, and only mine; for she has forgot 'ee at last,
although for her you died! But I – whenever I get up I'll
think of 'ee, and whenever I lie down I'll think of 'ee
again. . . . I'll think that none can plant as you planted;
and whenever I split a gad, and whenever I turn the
cider wring, I'll say none could do it like you. If ever I
forget your name let me forget home and heaven! . . .
But no, no, my love, I never can forget 'ee; for you was
a good man, and did good things!' (Chap. 48)

The lyrical love-lament is reminiscent in form and
language, harking back to the companionable work of
these woodlanders. Stronger than Henchard's in some
ways, Marty's imagination habitually recognizes human
nature as part of larger nature, in a green awareness present
in many of Hardy's imaginative characters. It is not
surprising that Marty's spontaneous sympathy for the
newly planted sighing pines is renewed, like Tess's
passions, by Hardy's poetry, in 'The Pine Planters' because
her prose leans towards poetry, alertly metaphorical, sensuous, harmonious and patterned, animated by the wood-
lander's personifications, rooted in knowledge: it is
because she knows the live feel and sound of trees that
she speaks of them as intimates.

Marty's imagination becomes central, but for large
stretches of *The Woodlanders* it is kept out of sight or plays
a subdued part. Transplanted to *Tess of the d'Urbervilles*
(1891) it is centred, concentrated, and developed. Tess is
not Marty but there is an affinity between the two
characters and their minds. In Tess the creative mind is

studied and dramatized afresh, developed in new forms, action and ideas. In her and for her Hardy imagines the growth of imagination most thoroughly and individually.

She and her novel conclude Hardy's exploration of mind in pastoral characters. Like Gabriel Oak, Henchard and Marty, Tess is imagined without condescension or sentimentality. She is made unromantically heroic. After her come Hardy's studies of Jude and Sue, modern intellectuals, informed and philosophically speculative. But Tess is no simple rustic girl. Like some of D. H. Lawrence's working-class characters, she is given enough education – in her case, up to Standard Six – to allow her to be socially bilingual. She is bookish enough to know, quote and revise the language and mythology of the Bible, peasant enough for folk-wisdom and folk-ignorance. She is unselfconscious enough to make up her own language, and is the most strikingly articulate of Hardy's characters, possessed of a creativity he does not repeat in the more conventional languages of Jude and Sue. Self-conscious and class-conscious about literary and artistic allusion, perhaps because he was such a highly educated auto-didact,[2] Hardy locates his best powers of language in a – relatively speaking – under-educated character, a milk-maid and farm-labourer.

From the beginning Tess speaks with a mastery of metaphor and symbol, rising above the expressive images of Gabriel Oak, Eustachia and Henchard. The night drive with Abraham when family fortunes start to decline, shows her capacity to transform familiar objects, like apples, in cosmic figuration. She is too easily seen as a mouthpiece for Hardy's pessimism. Of course she speaks for the author's purposes, like all fictional characters, but she is part of his effort to imagine life outside his own. The early speeches are first flowerings of her language, impelled by bitter intelligence. She feels intensely, and speaks her passions, like Henchard, without self-pity, but unlike him, from a generalizing and vivifying motion of mind able to separate the self that suffers and the self that speaks, imaging extensions and proofs of the family's pain, which in the circumstances have social implications she does not mention. The leap from apple to star, made in grievance but also as a natural explanation to her little brother, says it all. Her cry of pain is also communication.

Her symbolic acts are personal and inventive. She baptizes her baby in an innovative and rebellious remaking of ritual, like Henchard rethinking the idea of a will, and when she names the child 'Sorrow' she is assuming authority, a woman re-imagining herself as priest, and as Adam. Unlike Hardy's earlier characters, she has powers which expand and develop. Like Joyce's artist, she grows away from impulsive uncontrollable sexuality and from religion, into an able and occasionally confident recognition of the self in nature. (Like most women in her time and later, she cannot fly the nets of family, as Stephen Dedalus does.) Her imagination is able to impersonalize, relating – by link and distinction – her individual feelings to the natural world of which, like Gabriel and his descendant Tom Brangwen, she knows she is a part. She also knows it is larger than herself. She makes the connection with otherness which is imaginative, not fanciful, which Coleridge, definer of imagination, describes in *The Statesman's Manual* as creating a symbol 'consubstantial with the reality it represents'.

Unlike Jude, she has not been made self-conscious by education in pagan and rationalist, as well as Christian, culture, but she is pagan and rational. Tess also demonstrates the poetic ability Coleridge images in the *Biographia Literaria*, bringing 'the whole soul of man into activity'. The psyche of her male author is never so involved, and at the same time so analysed, as when he incarnates it in this female character's unspoilt expressiveness, unstereoty-ped, individual and intuitive but not untutored, unthink-ing or wild.

Angel is amused when they are waiting to load the milk on the London train and she talks about centurions, but she is in touch with the pagan and Christian strands in the culture. She questions Christianity, she describes an out-of-body experience, she is at home with the non-human animal world and the seasonal cycle, as she proves not only in sympathy but by re-enacting and articulating, as well as feeling, their vitality. Like the less schooled Gabriel and Marty she is a hardworking agricultural worker with knowledge and talent. Hardy knows the culture that shapes his pastoral figures and shows it enabling a holistic response to the natural world, in contemplation and the active forms of making and tending.

Hardy articulates Tess's creativity in a pure language – pure in being natural, unaffected, freely self-expressive and exploratory, and with the beauty of image and musical order. It is revealed as Tess develops, like the style and sensibility of Stephen Dedalus, though without Ste-phen's reading and revision. This is Hardy's portrait of the artist as a young countrywoman.

'But for the world's opinion', Tess's seduction, preg-nancy, and the death of her child, Hardy says at the beginning of the second Phase, 'Maiden no More' 'would have been simply a liberal education' (Chap. 15). A startling thing for a man, and a Victorian, to say about a woman, and an instance of Hardy's social daring. What does it mean?

Like Joyce, Hardy saw an intimate relation between sex and creativity, and in his novels sex and art interact causally and metaphorically. There is a certain shyness in his dealing with Tess, perhaps in the treatment of her rape-seduction, though he comes to relate her sensuousness to her creativity, as that develops in the course of a hampered but dynamic education. There are scenes in which Tess's sensations and emotions are shaped and self-shaping. Unlike the imagination imagined for the earlier creative characters, hers is plotted on a developmental curve.

She begins by reading her environment sensitively, simply and personally. In her night-walks during pregnancy her expedient choice of twilight is not just shown as timid but appraised as singular psychic response:

She knew how to hit to a hair's-breadth that moment of evening when the light and the darkness are so evenly balanced that the constraint of day and the suspense of night neutralize each other, leaving absolute mental liberty. It is then that the plight of being alive becomes attenuated to its least possible dimensions. (Chap. 13)

Hardy is one of the best Victorian psychologists of creativity because of his relaxed form and moral detachment: emotional and sensuous detail is common in other great Victorians, but usually instrumental to plot or moral: Jane Eyre's marsh and moor, Dombey's railway journey, Pendennis's high tide, Dorothea's sunsets and sunrise, Isabel Archer's shuttered house. Hardy keeps track of his plot, and makes scenes and objects work as moral symbols, but he can be fascinated by a discrete act of mind or feeling, like Coleridge in his notebook observations, and can free the scene from total relevance.

He is a scrupulous psychic observer. Perceptive as Tess is, the more informed narrator generalizing on her behalf places her perception as subjective, marking the imaginative process with which most Victorian novelists are simply complicit: 'Her . . . figure became an integral part of the scene', and:

At times her whimsical fancy would intensify the natural processes around her till they seemed a part of her
own story. Rather they became a part of it; for the
world is only a psychological phenomenon, and what
they seemed they were. (*loc. cit.*)

The qualification in the second sentence boldly dis-
penses with claims for metaphysical access. Analysis continues. After images of sympathetic nature in which
midnight gusts utter reproach and rain expresses 'irreme-
diable grief' on the part of 'some vague ethical being
whom she could not class definitely as the God of her
childhood and could not comprehend as any other', her
projection is criticized as mere projection, a recreation of
'mistaken fancy' 'based on shreds of convention'. Hardy
is showing the intellectual growth away from Christianity
as he coolly imagines the character's maturing imagination, and his anti-religious assumption is scarcely noticeable because it is so assimilated to critical portraiture.
    Tess grows away from her immature Christian fantasy
to feel free and open to nature, in a 'Rally' timed for
spring. 'She heard a pleasant voice in every breeze, and in
every bird's note seemed to lurk a joy' (Chap. 16). Her
fancy works in the old anthropocentric way, but Hardy's
preservative 'seemed' keeps 'heard' on the right and
rational side of imaginative activity, and the theme is
perception, not based not on Christian sin-ethic but on
the pleasure principle, 'the invincible instinct towards self-
delight' (Chap. 15) and the 'irresistible, universal, auto-
matic tendency to find sweet pleasure somewhere' (Chap.
16).
    Tess's perception widens and her mind grows. Personal
response becomes more complicated as she searches tradition for its articulations, first in 'several ballads', found
inadequate, then the book of Common Prayer:

'O ye Sun and Moon . . . O ye Stars . . . ye Green
Things upon the Earth . . . ye Fowls of the Air . . .
Beasts and Cattle . . . Children of Men . . . bless ye the
Lord, praise Him and magnify Him for ever!' (Chap.
16)

She needs to revise tradition, identifying with the praise
of delightful familiar nature all around her, but finding
the theology unacceptable, 'But perhaps I don't quite
know the Lord as yet'. (Lawrence follows this closely in
tracking Ursula Brangwen's growth away from Christianity in *The Rainbow*.) The cautious 'perhaps' and 'quite' are
followed by the didactic proposal that her 'half-uncon-
scious rhapsody' is probably a 'Fetishistic utterance in a
Monotheistic setting', characteristic of one 'whose chief
companions are the forms and forces of outdoor nature'.
Never trust the artist, trust the tale. Hardy might have
done better to let Tess speak for herself here, but that is
not his way. He wants to use his larger learning first to
place and support, the language of her mind. But the
informed narrator relaxes, and diegesis gives way to
drama.

We do not stray beyond the character's increasingly
sophisticated consciousness in the next two scenes of
imaginative articulation, whereTess responds to art and
nature. It is not great art, only the thin tones of Angel's
old second-hand harp, but heard out of doors on a
summer evening in the country. Her mind is privileged as
the creative authority, from her first moment of listening
to a voiced reponse. The shift from narrator to character
is marked. The narrator describes the June evening whose
'transmissive' atmosphere makes distinctions of space dis-
appear, then brings in 'an auditor' who 'felt close to
everything within the horizon', then moves from the
impersonal auditor to Tess, listening to silence, 'the

soundlessness impressed her as a positive entity rather than the mere negation of noise' and she takes over. Her response to the music, which she is competent to generalize as aesthetic experience, is prepared by her earlier account of her rapturous out-of-body experience, lying on the grass at night, looking 'straight up at some big bright star', and feeling 'you are hundreds and hundreds o' miles away from your body, which you don't seem to want at all' (Chap. 18). The free indirect style picks this up, but does not improve on it, because she has caught up with the narrator's analysis:

> Tess was conscious of neither time nor space. The exultation which she had described as being producible by will by gazing at a star, came now without any determination of hers. . . . The floating pollen seemed to be his notes made visible, and the dampness of the garden the weeping of the garden's sensibility. (Chap. 19)

This fancy, a secular version of the earlier religious projections, is sensuous, wonderfully kinaesthetic, and made provisional by 'seemed'.

After this sensitive narration comes a dialogue in which the originality of her language is contrasted with Angel's speech, which is literal-minded, 'the milk turning sour?', commonplace, 'Life in general', and seasoned only with educated slang: 'this hobble of being alive is rather serious', and 'any line of reading'. Though the narrator observes as 'rank-smelling' the 'weedflowers' to which she attributes 'intentness', all her words, sentences and dialect are as fresh as the spring season, the matrix of her imagery, 'the apple-blooth is falling, and everything is so green'. She thinks Angel musical and bookish, which he is, and poetic, which he is not, though his diction, syntax and imagery would not seem so flat without her vivid tentative figuration, lively questions and exclamations, and delicate rhythms:

> 'The trees have inquisitive eyes, haven't they? – that is, seem as if they had. And the river says, – "Why do ye trouble me with your looks?" And you seem to see numbers of to-morrows just all in a line, the first of them the biggest and clearest, the others getting smaller and smaller as they stand farther away; but they all seem very fierce and cruel and as if they said, "I'm coming! Beware of me!"' (*loc. cit.*)

She has left behind the pleasure principle of the spring rally but she has found more of her own language. She is no longer quoting but using her own rhetoric, grown adept in personification and dialogue, a better speaker. The language is guarded from within, the narrator's favourite 'seems', 'as if', and interrogations placed in her developed imagination and intelligence. The contrast between the star-story she tells to the workers, and these speeches, shows the ability to shift dialects, as the narrator notes. He has mentioned it before, but perhaps he is nervous here, and anxious to free her from an appearance of mere mouthpiece: 'her own native phrases – assisted a little by her Sixth Standard training'. Her lyricism, vivacity and intellectual care are striking, and in a nice touch Hardy makes the educated man struck by her 'touch of rarity' and her 'shaping' of 'imaginings'. Ignorantly surprised by such language from a village girl of – as he thinks – no experience, he blurs her into historical type, hearing her automatically utter 'the ache of modernism'. The narrator seems complicit, but detaches himself to correct Angel's 'no experience' with 'experience is as to intensity, and not as to duration', and hark back to the liberal education, 'Tess's passing corporeal blight had been her mental harvest' (Chap. 19).

Hardy has never been so thorough or explicit about any other character's creativity. Tess's imaginative language, and its contexts, are chronicled in detail and seen from several points of view, hers, Angel's, the narrator's, and behind them the author's.

This scene is repeated with variation, a few pages later. There is the same interrogation, the same lyrical searching dark speech, the same intensifying repetition, the same contrast, the same sensuous impulse from nature. The difference is in the vision's tense: Tess is talking about the past not the future. She is made more aware of social context, rebuked into a sharp particular sense of class and gender as she compares her opportunities with Angel's. He patronizes her language, she feels put down by his knowledge. The disadvantage of gender is brought out as she performs the unconscious symbolic action of picking flowers, lords and ladies, and commenting, 'there are always more ladies than lords'. But everything else she says is fully conscious, and her lamentation is powerful:

'Just a sense of what it might have been with me! My life looks as if it had been wasted for want of chances! When I see what you know, what you have read, and seen, and thought, I feel what a nothing I am! I'm like the poor Queen of Sheba who lived in the Bible. There is no more spirit in me'.

That lament, with its gauche, original, precise and accurate, 'lived in the bible', better than conventional phrasing, and its assimilated, first-person, quotation of a Queen's rebuked genius, shows she has her literary culture too, in spite of what she is saying. (A few paragraphs before she has joined Job and Bunyan.) Her style is enriched by her reading, more vivid, resonant and ordered than the dull, stiff, jerky and banal language of the university student who answers her poetry with the well-meaning Victorian offer of tutorial assistance, to 'help her' to 'anything in the way of history, or any line of reading', or 'any course of study'. The offer provokes a poetry of anger, rhetorically similar to her poetry of dread and grief:

'The best is not to remember that your nature and your past doings have been like thousands' and thousands', and that your coming life and doings 'll be like thousands' and thousands''.

She astonishes the clever well-read man by refusing to learn anything except what is philosophically relevant: 'I shouldn't mind learning why — why the sun do shine on the just and the unjust alike. . . . But that's what books will not tell me'. Books have instructed her thoughts and words, and she re-imagines the history, narrative, characters and language of her reading to articulate a rich sense of self and society, even in despair — like Thomas Hardy.

Later, her imagination re-voices the connection with the natural world when she discovers wounded birds left by the shoot, companions in insult and injury. She transforms her personal pain in love, and as she carries out her tender killing as toughly as a farm-woman could, the dialect she speaks to the birds is simple, ancient, musical in order and repetition. The episode is compassionate and completely unsentimental. She is unselved:

'Poor darlings — to suppose myself the most miserable being on earth in the sight o' such misery as yours!' she exclaimed, her tears running down as she killed the birds tenderly. 'And not a twinge of bodily pain about me. I be not mangled, and I be not bleeding; and I have two hands to feed and clothe me'. (Chap. 41)

She is to prove that will to survive with those two strong hands, when she is forced by poverty to go back to Alec, kill less tenderly, and be hanged.

Before the novel ends, with her end, she is imagined in one further flight of imagination. Like Henchard, but at the end not the beginning of her tragedy, she imagines the ultimately desirable but impossible – freedom and the unconditional. In Bramshurst, the happy house, furnished but uninhabited, the novel finds its fantastic image of social isolation and shelter, like Lear's prison, where she and Angel briefly live alone in honeymoon and marriage. The image is so powerful that the question of a sexual consummation is neither here nor there. Even the murder briefly stops being an issue. Hardy does not cut her off quickly or inhumanely, and she repents her crime, but Angel significantly does not know whether she has actually committed it or not, even when she says: 'Yet formerly I never could bear to hurt a fly or a worm, and the sight of a bird in a cage used often to make me cry' (Chap. 58).

This follows the pure impossible dream of the escape from time, history and contingency, the constraints she has experienced and articulated so imaginatively and realistically. Time stops. The distant and immediate past of murder and marriage is excluded. She shuts off her vision of the threatening tomorrows though as she speaks we are aware of them:

> 'Don't think of what's past!' said she, 'I am not going to think outside of now! Why should we? Who knows what tomorrow has in store?' (Chap. 58)

This Phase is entiled 'Fulfilment', and the title is not wholly ironic. As Tess peeps outside to say, 'All is trouble outside there; inside here content', her sense of release and holiday offers fulfilment through imagination. She rests briefly cocooned, within her virtually finished story and inexorable history. Angel's desire has crystallized round her image and his conventional image of woman, but he is forced to share her dream of respite. He takes an imaginative leap, responding spontaneously, impelled to love as her love purely expects, 'Tenderness . . . dominant', the possible crime dismissed with 'anyhow', the whispered telling in the lovers' night not about murder but of 'how he walked in his sleep with her in his arms'.

Like Henchard, Tess speaks tragically for herself and her destruction, but unlike him she is allowed to imagine a better self, as well as a better life. Her powers of shaping and speaking are enlarged, and unlike Hardy' s other finely articulate and articulated characters – except for Jude – she makes explicit the growing points of the novel, and of Hardy's own imagination, pressing against the limits of personal and social possibilities. Perhaps she represents the artist better than Jude, who begins by imagining poetically but applies a conventionally educated control, to represent Hardy's rational and philosophical impulse. Jude, like his author, is a highly self-educated man, and perhaps his education inhibits his dreaming of freedom and the unconditional. (Clym Yeobright, the educated man who returns to nature, is I think Hardy's only other character to imagine the unconditional, which he does in a quick dream with the aid of moonlight.)

It is a dream Hardy can dream through the mediating imagination of Tess. In the Preface to *Wessex Poems*, he speaks of feeling freer as a poet than as a novelist, and the concept of creative freedom is useful when we think of Tess. She is freed – freer than a middle-class highly educated man like Angel – from the apparatus and style of rational and philosophical speculation, and the conventional culture of learning, freer to find a language of her own, to imagine beyond history and culture, at least for a short time, in a small space. Like Jude she is close to

Hardy the narrative artist but also close to Hardy the lyrical poet. She is the pure artist as well as the pure woman, a character inside Hardy's book capable of being its best reader, even its writer,[3] able by the end to articulate its characters, courses and conclusions, though imagined as different and other.

CHAPTER THREE

Good times in Jude the Obscure: *Constructing Fictions*

There are good times in *Jude the Obscure*, carefully constructed as parts of the novel's pattern and as images
created by the characters. The good times are mostly for
Jude, but sometimes for Jude and Sue – leading lovers and
exemplary characters – together. They are really good
times, the best on offer by nature and culture. They are
not mocked, distored or ambiguous, like the dubious
consolations in Samuel Beckett, or minimal, like the
'minute forms of satisfaction' Elizabeth-Jane Farfrae makes
the most of in *The Mayor of Casterbridge* or the little props
and stays ('*die Hilfskonstruktionen*') famously recommended
in Fontane's *Effie Briest*, published the year before *Jude* in
1895. Hardy's good times are substantial experiences, of
content, happiness, joy, bliss and ecstasy, and mostly
shown in vividly particularized detail. I began with a
count of about half a dozen but I keep finding more. The
occasions I discuss are unmistakably happy, and often last
for a long time, both in narrative time and time narrated.
They occur of course in a fictional action where good
times are notoriously scarce, bad times frequent, and
where the central couple, as well as many other characters,
are often in positive pain.

What is the interest of these good times, imagined in
this novel? I want to counter the common view of a
novel teeming with unrelieved gloom and doom, and also
to correct a judgement of my own, made in *The Appropriate Form* (1964) where I argued that Hardy's tragic novels

were dogmatic forms, too realistic for a fable but too schematically illustrative for realism, and dogmatically expressive. While admitting that Hardy's novelistic psychology was animated and realistic – it was hard to discuss the novel 30 years ago without mentioning realism – I believed that *Jude the Obscure* was characteristically ideological, constructing a didactic pattern, a game of Snakes and Ladders which was all snakes and no ladders. I saw Hardy's major novels, apart from *Far from the Madding Crowd*, as anti-Providence novels, reversing the simple exemplary Christian patterning of Daniel Defoe and Charlotte Brontë but forming a similar stereotyped action.

I believe now that the novel is too intelligently self-aware for such dogmatic simplification. As schematic construction it is self-exposed, its arguments and illustrations complicated by Hardy's fundamental theme of imagination and imaginative construction. As an anti-Providence novel, it is totally aware of the simplifications of the Providence novel, parodies them, plays with them, overrides them and avoids them.

Hardy's delineation of good times makes a text and a context for destruction and frustration, but presents tragedy as common and likely, neither eccentric nor pathological. The good times have some philosophical interest too, as episodes of imagined freedom from contingency, time, history and necessity. Both the placing of internal narrations, and the emotional emphasis on the good times and happy days, show Hardy's art as complex, sophisticated, and self-conscious enough to discover counter-themes and forms of reflexivity.

The first set of good times in *Jude* is created by internal narrative, subversive and reflexive in fable and fiction. We begin with Jude's dreams. He wishes and hopes passionately, and his gratifying fantasies are clearly shaped as inset narratives. This inner story-telling occurs in all novels, as mimesis, function and microcosm, and though of course it plays a part in the psychological portraiture and motivation of the characters, it also places, emphasizes and reflects on Hardy's tragically illustrative action and argument. The novel's form is not dogmatic: on the contrary, it frames a dogmatic fable provisionally and tentatively, within a consciousness – primarily that of Jude – which is itself tentative, preserving the novel as a whole from authoritarian and absolutist claims. As we read the story and the stories within it we are consistently shown the character's narratives, chiefly Jude's, but also Sue's, Phillotson's, Arabella's, Drusilla Fawley's and others'. The narratives alert us to the modes and motives of narrative in general, for life and art, they concentrate, like many novels of the last two centuries, on wish-fulfilment fantasies, and some of them particularize forms of fable, even the special genre of providence-fiction.

Hardy hated to be labelled as pessimistic, indeed, as systematic and dogmatic, claiming that his writings were not arguments but impressions or seemings. And yet everyone would agree that his novels are severe on the providence novel, and in turning it on its head are anti-providence fictions. Perhaps the most lucid way of reconciling his laid-back claim to impressionism is to look at his proliferation of micro-narratives. Jude begins as a solitary adolescent bookish dreamer, like many characters in fiction, and his dreams are bruised and broken by personal and social injustice. His naïve childlike faith in Christminster, inspired by the influential model of Phillotson's ideal and aim, is also backed by rumour and hearsay, like the aspiring fantasy of the hunchbacked old woman 'of great intelligence', and less informed gossip and local legend on the fringe of the university city. Unlike Don Quixote's and Catherine Morland's, Jude's story-telling is not rooted in literary romance, though some part is played by biblical texts, Bunyan, and Latin poetry. Various strands and influences create a dominant fable, sustained and revised throughout the novel.

The construction of narrative is emphasized from the beginning. Jude's visions are made sensuously substantial, but they are presented as visions being formed, traditionally, individually, and plausibly but also ambiguously. He sees the visions in a natural location which is throughly poeticized, by novelist and characters. In Chapter Two and Three of Part One Jude climbs to a green ridgeway, 'the Icknield Street and original Roman road', then from it to a better height for his Pisgah-sight, up a workman's ladder from which the view is sometimes obscured. (The relevance of Hardy's fine detail is not perhaps as total as George Eliot's or Henry James's but it is extensive.) Jude strains his eyes to see Christminster and is stimulated by the roof-tiler's occupation, and by his uncompleted comparison: 'The time I've noticed it is when the sun is going down in a blaze of flame, and it looks like – I don't know what'. When Jude suggests 'The heavenly Jerusalem,' the tiler agrees, 'Ay – though I should never ha' thought of it myself'. (This is one of Hardy's small significant narrative collaborations: it contributes to the class fable and the lament for obscured genius.)

All this before Jude sees anything of the distant city. After the workmen leave he climbs again and prays, because he recalls along with a couple of 'not discouraging' anecdotes, how 'People said that, if you prayed, things sometimes came to you, even though they sometimes did not'. He sensibly prays a short-term prayer for the mist to rise, and it does, in the west, making him look backwards, north-east, at reflected points of sunlight showing themselves as 'vanes, windows, wet roof slates' and other architectural detail of spires, domes and city outlines: 'Christminster, unquestionably; either directly seen, or miraged in the peculiar atmosphere'. The last nine words did not appear in *Harper's Magazine* where the first edition of the novel was serialized as *The Simpletons*. but were added subsequently, destabilizing but not destroying the vision. In the free indirect narrative, they merge the narrator's qualification and hesitancy with Jude's. They also show Hardy's attention to the passage. As Jude leaves, darkness makes shapes monstrous and evokes frightening stories: 'He knew that he had grown out of belief in these horrors, yet he was glad when he saw the church tower . . .'. Still childlike, but showing growth, and awareness of the growth. (And Hardy gently touches on one use of religion.)

For much of these first chapters Jude makes a continuous narrative out of tradition, text, and oral story, combining fantasy with 'the air of reality (solidity of specification)' which Henry James emphasizes in the best contemporary discussion of the novel, 'The Art of Fiction' (1884).[1] Hardy emphasizes not mimesis, but 'tangibility', 'permanence' and 'hold on his life', all characteristic of his image of the city, 'mainly from the one nucleus of fact that the man for whose knowledge and purpose he had so much reverence was actually living there' (Bk I, Chap. 3). That 'nucleus of fact' significantly merges into Jude's fiction, though the fiction is not outrageous: 'not only so, but living among the more thoughtful and mentally shining ones'. Hardy is showing the flux and reflux of the idealizing imagination – a touch of it in the metaphor 'shining' – amid a sense of the real. He specifies the style of Jude's imagination and his revision of text and tradition, and there are more fine details in his sense of the barrier which does not impede Jude's vision, and also in his dry sideglance at Apocalyptic imagery, typical of the way he divides his attention, between the development of his hero and the sub-text of his own scepticism:

Through the solid barrier of cold cretaceous upland to
the northward he was always beholding a gorgeous city
– the fancied place he had likened to the new Jerusalem, though there was perhaps more of the painter's
imagination, and less of the diamond merchant's in his
dreams thereof than in those of the Apocalyptic writer.
(Bk I, Chap. 3)

When Jude re-enacts his sunset vision at night to get a
view of the city lights he sees a 'halo or glow-fog' instead
of the individual lamps he expects, and adjusts his fantasy
to the new unexpected feature. The language is as always
tentative, the vision a seeming not a certainty: 'he seemed
to see Phillotson' and he draws on the Old Testament: 'to
see Phillotson promenading at ease, like one of the forms
in Nebuchadnezzar's furnace'.

His fantasy is also grounded – consciously – in science,
as he apostrophizes the breezes from the north-east in the
knowledge that 'breezes travelled at the rate of ten miles
an hour'. Addressing them 'caressingly' – the adverb seems
pleasantly role-reversing and may or may not be a relic of
an earlier intention to have Sue and not Phillotson in
Christminster at the time – he imagines a reply, balancing
romance and reality:

Suddenly there came along this wind something
towards him – a message from the place – from some
soul residing there, it seemed. Surely it was the sound
of bells, the voice of the city; faint and musical, calling
to him, 'We are happy here!' (*loc. cit.*)

There is rational caution and surmise in 'some',
'seemed', 'surely' and fantasy in 'soul', 'voice' and the
happy message. At the end of the chapter Jude sums up
his vision in an endearingly pedantic list of idealizing
metaphors, all traditional, biblical, particular to his experi-

ence and eloquent of his joy: 'city of light', 'tree of knowledge', 'teachers of men', and, with one hint of provisionality in his most sophisticated figure, 'It is what you may call a castle, manned by scholarship and religion'. In the *Harper's* serial the castle is called 'sublime' and Hardy's slight desublimation reduces the possibility of either irony or overstatement. The summing-up of elated hope is simple, colloquial and beautiful, 'It would just suit me'.

This good time of happiness grows over several episodes. In the next chapter generalized hope becomes particular. Vilbert promises his old Greek and Latin grammars and during a specified fortnight between promise and disappointment, Jude's great happiness is summarized in a vivid passage:

> Through the intervening fortnight he ran about and smiled outwardly at his inward thoughts, as if they were people meeting and nodding to him – smiled with that singularly beautiful irradiation which is seen to spread on young faces at the inception of some glorious idea, as if a supernatural lamp were held inside their transparent natures, giving rise to the flattering fancy that heaven lies about them then. (Bk 1, Chap. 4)

There is a joining of outside and inside, which makes an impact by jumping the usual gap between appearance and reality, so that the sign of smiling is lit by the state of joy, emotion really matching expression. Affirmation is not afraid of superlatives, 'singularly beautiful'. Jude's activity is doubled, 'ran about and smiled', and the animation of his thoughts 'like people meeting and nodding to him' is strongly responsive to the vigour and companionableness of joy. Old and new light images come together, 'irradiation,' 'glorious' and 'lamp . . . held inside . . . transparent natures'. The passage is full of conceits expressing young vivacious happiness, and though it abruptly ends with the ironic, scornful and neatly assimilated allusion to Wordsworth's 'Ode on the Intimations of Immortality in Childhood', the good time still makes itself felt. Joy reaches such a high point that its existence is not spoilt or cancelled, reminding me of something Patrick Kavanagh says about tragedy, that there is something false about it, because it is the comic which marks the abundance of life. That abundance is what Hardy registers, for a while.

Another feeling of young joy is not directly connected with the dream of Christminster, though it helps to substantiate that heartbreaking dream, and makes it more gratuitously inappropriate to suggest, as two Oxford scholars[2] have, that his academic aspirations were misplaced and he was better off as a stone-mason. Jude is wrong to believe that he can conquer Casterbridge, but quite right in his dream of learning, as every scholar who enjoys scholarship should agree. He comes into the full intellectual and emotional privilege of that learning, matching nature with literature. As he drives his baker's cart, he is moved by sunset coinciding with moonrise, and draws on Horace for celebration. He finds that nature can authenticate poetry, that poetry has helped him feel nature. Three things meet to make a passionate moment, a true ecstasis, a going-out of self. Nature, classical poetry and youth come together in what I do not call an epiphany, since Jude's experience is too particularized to be labelled by the religious image Joyce wittily secularized and started off on a career as a cover-all cliché. In this scene no one single thing is manifested. Many things are coming together:

> On a day when Fawley was getting quite advanced, being now about sixteen, and had been stumbling through the 'Carmen Saeculare', on his way home, he

found himself to be passing over the high edge of the plateau by the Brown House. The light had changed, and it was the sense of this which had caused him to look up. The sun was going down, and the full moon was rising simultaneously. . . . His mind had become so impregnated with the poem that, in a moment of the same impulsive emotion which years before had caused him to kneel on the ladder, he stopped the horse, alighted, and glancing round to see that nobody was in sight, knelt down on the roadside bank with open book. He turned first to the shiny goddess, who seemed to look so softly and critically at his doings, then to the disappearing luminary on the other hand, as he began: 'Phoebe silvarumque potens Diana!' (Bk 1, Chap. 5)

It ought to be a famous moment of vision, like Stephen Dedalus seeing the wading girl (also an initiation deepened by an allusion to an image of Venus in Latin poetry[3]), or Mrs Ramsay at her dinner table. Like them, it is the poetry of fiction, one of many moments in Hardy which make us drop the comparison of his achievements in the two genres. It is a moving coincidence of literature and experience, and pays homage to both in an act of nature-worship made poignantly pedagogic, as the boy's hard solitary classical grind turns out to have empowered such response to art and nature. 'Impregnated by the poem' as poets and their critics want readers to be, he is the vehicle for Hardy's homage to Horace, the poet so congenial to him in scepticism, irony, resignation and passion. In the sublime natural scene, doubling day and night, sun and moon, Hardy anticipates one of Yeats's images of perfection and unity of being, writes a scene of secular bliss, and demonstrates that Jude the obscure has learnt to read and appreciate classical poetry.

Jude is sixteen and Horace wrote this Ode for a pagan festival, the Secular Games, to be sung by a choir of boys

and girls in the Temple of Apollo. This is also an
adolescent rite, renewed as ritual must be, for this individual boy or man, this particular culture, shyly and in
solitude. And dangerously. The word 'impregnated' is apt
and daring for the rite, and for Horace's Ode, ironically
attached to Jude's future by its wishes for fertility and
parenthood. Instead of taking the ritual as a sensual
initiation Jude is alerted to his own susceptibility to
paganism and polytheism, and decides to check it: 'there
seemed little harmony between this pagan literature and
the mediaeval colleges of Christminster', but he has
invoked dangerous powers. The occasion is a moment of
vision and temporarily gains strength as it discredits the
Christian, the mediaeval, and the romantic.

There is a flashback to the earlier visions of the city,
where light was important. Though the narrative does not
say so, this moonrise blots out the previous reflected
sunset glow in the east, to suggest an alternative instance.
The incident's particularity overrides the sense of recall or
repetition, taking us on not back. Later on, Sue, for a
time ahead of Jude in cultural and intellectual development, substitutes the god, of Jude's Horatian ode, Apollo
with Venus, for Christian saints, and this scene anticipates
her period of hellenism and pagan joy, playing a part in
the novel's covert attack on the pale Galilean, from whom
Sue and Jude cannot synchronize their liberation. The act
of pagan worship stands apart from Jude's main constructed narrative, or relates to it as a deviation which is
corrected. Jude is the receiver, not the creator, here giving
way to Horace and his gods. But though this is a rite
learnt from literature, it is also the spontaneous motion of
wonder, at nature made strange and poetry made natural.
This is the story and the poetry Jude should have articulated. Ironically, he decides to turn from the pagan to the
Christian values, rejecting Horace and the secular games.

In Jude's sentimental progress, Hardy shows the

delighted vision, the blissful hope, the celebration of youth, nature, art, then the joy of sex. His gratified desire for Arabella is a coarse and unscrupulous marriage-seduction by the woman and an interruption of the man's ambitious course. But it is also the powerful new experience of sexual desire and satisfaction. Hardy deplores the instrument and the tragic social and psychological results, but he tells the truth about the pleasure principle. He dramatizes the seduction harshly, and relatively speaking, grossly. He demystifies and standardizes Jude's response bluntly, in contemptuous military metaphors, as 'obedience to conjunctive orders from headquarters'. He shows Jude's unresistant response to the imperative authority, but at the same time makes his hero see the arbitrariness of desire and object, with the 'intellectual eye' but makes it clear that the desire is a source of delight: 'Jude was lost to all conditions of things in the advent of a fresh and wild pleasure' (Bk 1, Chap. 6). He finds a perfect image for the freshness and wildness, 'he felt as a snake must feel who has sloughed off its winter skin, and cannot understand the brightness and sensitiveness of its new one'. The seduction and marriage are shown so squalidly and drably that the sensations may be forgotten – how many Victorian novelists register the sexual thrill like this, or at all? As with his account of Jude's young blissful hopefulness Hardy makes the pleasure felt with a shock of imagery, getting into and out of a snake's skin to register sexual excitement and its amazing novelty for a virgin.

Hardy obviously loved writing about desire, and having his fling in what turned out to be his last novel, and a very shocking one, he found it necessary to do so, because Victorian readers were often told that what was bad for you was repulsive. Hardy did not tell that kind of story. Dickens's repulsive sexuality, in Quilp or Pecksniff, is exciting, but he never showed anyone simply enjoying sex, and most of the novelists left out sexual pleasure or showed it very indirectly. Hardy is probably the first English novelist to image the fresh wild pleasure of young sex. (He was also excited by its dark side.)

There is a good long wait for Jude's next good experience. When he first arrives in Christminster his imagination is active, and Hardy draws attention to his construction and selection: he wanders, 'encircled, as it were with the breadth and sentiment of the venerable city', and 'When he passed objects out of harmony with its general expression he allowed his eyes to slip over them as if he did not see them' (Bk 2, Chap. 1). Jude's reading and knowledge invoke a band of eloquent Christminster worthies as 'comrades in his solitude', but the episode is not one shown as pleasing Jude. Hardy concentrates on the grand solemn chorus, once or twice interrupted or checked by Jude's fancy, but here he neglects Jude's feelings. The morning after is said to replace 'what at night had been perfect and ideal' with what 'was by day the more or less defective real', but Jude's excitement has been taken for granted and not shown. Later on, his disillusion and bitter disappointment and disapproval are registered strongly but for some reason – too overwhelming an experience for author and character? too tempting for Hardy to put his imaginary chorus in the foreground? – the pleasure of arriving at the ideal city, his castle, is left out.

Jude's construction of the Christminster story in Christminster only becomes pleasurable when academic ambition is joined by desire for Sue. Like Christminster, she is imagined and loved before she is seen, then she is merely seen. Jude's fancy prepares her image, then constructs their story. Hardy is clear about its process. He traces the story-telling to the 'bottled-up effect of solitude and the poeticized locality' and shows Jude once more narrating with care, trying to control the shapes of desire: 'he would have to think of Sue with only a relation's

mutual interest in one belonging to him; regard her in a
practical way' (Bk 2, Chap. 2). As he sets out a rational
scenario, it gets out of hand, in spite of tea and the
Church of England: he will regard her in a practical way
'as some one to be proud of; to talk and nod to; later on,
to be invited to tea by, the emotion spent on her being
rigorously that of a kinsman and well-wisher' (*loc. cit.*).
The thought of rigour is suspect, and the story intensifies,
in spite of his attempts at control: 'So would she be to
him a kindly star, an elevating power, a companion in
Anglican worship, a tender friend'.

Seeing Sue in church, just as he hoped, he assimilates
into his story the chanting of the 119th Psalm, 'Where-
withal shall a young man cleanse his way?':

> The great waves of pedal music tumbled round the
> choir, and, nursed on the supernatual as he had been, it
> is not wonderful that he could hardly believe that the
> psalm was not specially set by some regardful Provi-
> dence for this moment of his first entry into the solemn
> building. (Bk 2, Chap. 3)

Tender observation and inference make their contribution, and the character of Sue is constructed, as the free
indirect style slyly registers. Hardy indicates the causes of
Jude's fantasy, and Jude does some imaginary psychologis-
ing on his part:

> The girl for whom he was beginning to nourish an
> extraordinary tenderness, was at this time ensphered by
> the same harmonies as those which floated into his ears;
> and the thought was a delight to him. She was probably
> a frequenter of this place, and, steeped body and soul
> in church sentiment as she must be by occupation and
> habit, had, no doubt, much in common with him. (*loc.
> cit.*)

Letting fantasy develop, Hardy makes it plain that his plot is not providential – 'it was the ordinary psalm for the twenty-fourth evening of the month' – but Jude persists for some time in thinking he is the hero of a Providence novel. He starts with self-delighting and optimistic constructions but he can incorporate less pleasant experience too. When Sue summons him to Melchester because she hates her training college he sees the very stones as signs. Once again, while Hardy develops Jude he is cool about superstitious Christianity – as if he cannot wait for Jude to catch up with him:

> He took it as a good omen that numerous blocks of stone were lying about, which signified that the cathedral was undergoing restoration or repair. . . . It seemed to him, full of the superstitions of his beliefs, that this was an exercise of forethought on the part of a ruling Power, that he might find plenty to do in the art he practised while waiting for a call to higher labours. (Bk 3, Chap. 1)

When Arabella returns from Australia and the past, and he spends a night with her instead of keeping an appointment with Sue, his remorse is softened by the thought, 'Arabella was perhaps an intended intervention to punish him for his unauthorized love'. But at last the Providence novel becomes hard to construct, and when an invitation from Sue arrives too late, there are signs of strain, which he himself observes, as he follows the old form, and between the two sentences that follow, he finally gives it up:

> at last his chimerical expedition to Kennetbridge really did seem to have been another special intevention of Providence to keep him away from temptation. But a growing impatience of faith, which he had noticed in

himself more than once of late, made him pass over in ridicule the idea that God sent people on fools' errands. (Bk 3, Chap. 10)

Here he flouts the providential pattern while still sounding devout, but when Sue asks how his 'heart' could go back to Arabella, his reply, 'A special providence, I suppose, helped it on its way' (Bk 4, Chap. 1) is bitterly irreverent. The unchristian omniscient narrator can relax now: Jude says it all for him. Increasingly aware of his own processes, he is finding out that he is in an anti-Providence novel and from now on he revises old narratives to create new ones which are microcosms of *Jude the Obscure*, and not about good times at all.

At the end it is Sue Bridehead, the free spirit and free thinker, who re-constructs the Providence novel, imposing a terrible restriction and law on her behaviour and her body. Hardy does not make Sue's consciousness central, and we mostly learn about her mind and imagination through her conversations with Jude. Her ideological turnabout is encouraged, if not totally motivated, by her sexual fears and coldness. Not totally motivated: of course Sue's experience of poverty and social injustice is part of what drives her back to Christian and conservative law and order, but her frigidity seems too conveniently to merge with a religious masochism. It is by no means an implausible character, and her terrible loss of the children stands for actual social experience, but Hardy may have been motivated by personal experience, or an early mistrust of feminism, to make not so much a new woman, but a woman ill-at-ease with her physicality. (The scene at the rose show, discussed at the end of this chapter, shows her in a different light.)

The reader's lack of access to her inner life increases the feeling that she is made an example of a tragedy running parallel to Jude's, and diminished by the instrumentality. Hardy had to separate this pair, almost too well imagined as elective affinities. In the end Sue not only imagines a terrible plot for Providential revenge, but shapes her behaviour accordingly, 'We must conform!'. She cannot accept what she is told by Jude, now close to his author, that they are not fighting against God but 'only against man and senseless circumstance' (Bk 6, Chap. 3). Her rationalism is not all that easily lost, and she briefly acquiesces, 'True!. . . . I am getting as superstitious as a savage!', but to be terribly cowed into living out the old fantasy.

The new story makes Jude a destroyed tragic hero, though there is perhaps just a suggestion that he survives, as in historical terms he does, outside fiction, to haunt still the exclusive and excluding walls that are such prominent images in the great extra-mural novel. One actual good time is present in Jude's half-heard, half-imagined story, 'I hear that soon there is going to be a better chance for such helpless students. . . . schemes . . . for making the University less exclusive, and extending its influence,' (Bk 6, Chap. 10). Jude and Hardy set the tragedy of educational deprivation – a part of a larger social tragedy of class – in the context of the then current hopes for the University Extension movement, and Jude's 'extending' may echo that politically significant word.

Neither Jude's revision of the providential story nor Sue's reversion to it are happy. They are hideous conclusions to the earlier delights which they misinterpret. Many of their good times are illusory or mistakenly interpreted. The most solid moment of bliss, Jude's matching of nature, sexuality, poetry and learning in his celebration of Apollo of the woods and great Diana, has a dark sub-text as well as a Horatian one of secular joy – the deities invoked were dangerous gods, one jealous of art and the other of desire. The experience itself is neither

illusory nor invalidated, Hardy lets it stand without retro-
spect or revision. Jude's youthful happiness in desire, faith
and ambition is neither illusory nor invalidated. The
stories he projects from these emotions and ideals are
illusory, but the experiences are real imaginary glimpses
of a freedom which cannot yet or perhaps ever be
socialized.

The tragic lovers have a few good times together, as
most lovers do. Continuation or renewal is not guaran-
teed, but the good experiences are not completely cut off
from past and future, and the connections are important
in a novel which thwarts desire, consummation and
fertility so thoroughly and cruelly. As well as preserving
the inquiry into history and imagination – Hardy's great
themes – from lapsing into diagram and scheme, the good
times familiarize the plot and action. Victor Shklovsky[4]
reminds us of what Coleridge said more simply a century
before, that art makes experience strange but the counter-
truth, which Coleridge also stated, needs re-stating: art
also makes experience ordinary and familiar. Some of the
good times in this hard novel – it is not as hard as life
though – make the life lived in its pages seem customary,
usual, everyday. So more terrifying, piteous and
illustrative.

The novel becomes reflexive as fiction and as fable,
largely through its structure of narratives. Their tragic
illuminations are extended by a proliferation of bad times
in these inset stories, for instance, the Fawley family
histories of bad marriage, and the implicit histories of the
couples encountered in the registry office. But these tales
of doom are accompanied by the stories of better times,
presented as holidays and excursions from the tragic
experience for which the novel is heading from its first
page, and before which, as Hardy said, his imagination
became vocal. He includes, however, as bright shadows,

the experience before which his nature generally did not become vocal, registering both its existence and his tendentious selection.

The imaginative survey of fictions does not take place solely in the internal story-telling. Taking the theme of good times as link, we see that some of the directly narrated and dramatic episodes also show some reflexive action, and are far from naïve and unmediated.

Hardy's presentation of experience centres on Jude, and through him on the transient self-delighting forms of desire. But his action is also concerned with more 'solid joys', though not with what the hymn calls divine 'lasting pleasures'. These all concern Sue, and her relationship with Jude. The reader is not given direct access to Sue's consciousness, which we read in her direct speech, infer from her actions and to some extent from other characters: so the dramatizations in which she figures are crucial. There are three prolonged episodes of satisfaction for the couple, and their weight must be recognized, in spite of and because of the tragic deaths of their children, the possible lack of sexual pleasure, and their final separation and destruction, one in death, the other in living.

Their love and union has an origin in fantasy, seen in the providential narrative, appearing as what Stendhal in *L'Amour* famously described as crystallisation. It is more than fantasy, because of their affinity and because they feel for each other as individuals not appropriated objects of desire. Hardy uses the happy episodes in the love story, like Jude's moment of vision, to imagine the common dream of escape from history, a dream the more pathetic and creative because of its ordinary substantiality in actual event. These experiences are of social and cultural pleasures, experienced and intensified, but not mutated or sublimated, by human love. The word holiday is a secularization of a religious celebration, and Hardy acknowledges that where relevant.

The first occasion is formally announced: 'Tomorrow is our grand day, you know' (Bk 3, Chap. 2). The outing is in strong contrast with the many spoiled treats, parties and picnics in fiction – in Jane Austen, Thackeray, Henry James, Fontane, Scott Fitzgerald – and is entirely successful. A good time is had from beginning to end, though like all good things it has to end. It is eagerly anticipated on its eve, with all the excitement of shared planning and choosing: 'Where shall we go?' and 'Not ruins, Jude – I don't care for them'. There is friendship here, fun and freedom in the air.

But the outing has a time-frame round it: 'I have leave from three till nine. Wherever we can get to . . . in that time'. It is a proper holiday, a break, a recess, an intermission, a period out of time, a time-tabled freedom. Jude feels, 'Every detail of the outing was a facet reflecting a sparkle,' and 'he did not venture to meditate on the life of inconsistency he was leading'. The lovers plan, but get times and distances wrong, miss their train and don't get home till morning. Neither the pleasures nor the sense of living in the moment make this outing a Bakhtinian carnival. It is only a holiday, with the perfect holiday's relaxation, release, and amusement. Louis Macneice's 'Epilogue' in *The Earth Compels* gets it right, 'Holidays should be like this / Free from over-emphasis'.

Hardy gets it right too, making the occasion neither a crisis, like Emma's Boxhill picnic, nor a plot crisis, like the dinner party where Dorothea meets Casaubon, nor a symbol, like the Waterloo ball in *Vanity Fair*. This holiday, and some of the others in this novel, are ordinary, small-scale occasions carefully rooted in the social culture, and that is their point. Unextravagant pleasure makes holiday as important as the exotic carnival, and may be, like carnival, a sign and indicator of release. In Jude there is enjoyment and an air of freedom, not abandon or license, and the lovers behave decorously. Hardy sometimes suggests that human beings may not ask for much in the way of happiness, and though they may not get much, they get a little.

Small pleasures accumulate, as at the beginning of this journey, done in one sentence where punctuation lightens and phrases rush, to catch the train and the excitement and bustle of travel:

> There duly came the charm of calling at the College door for her ; her emergence in a nunlike simplicity of costume that was rather enforced than desired; the traipsing along to the station, the porter's "B'your leave!", the screaming of the trains – everything formed the basis of a beautiful crystallization.[5]

To arrive is as good as to journey, and the cultural visit to Wardour Castle – 'a classic building – Corinthian, I think; with a lot of pictures' – lightly touches on Jude's taste for religious art and Sue's for profane, but is good-natured, uncontentious, free and easy.

After culture comes nature, and the couple decide to take what they think is a short-cut between stations and walk 'across the high country', Sue inclining to 'adventure' and enjoying 'the sense of her day's freedom'. The route is descriptively mapped, then dramatized in a 'bounding walk' and intelligent conversation. Sue and Jude are remarkably like a pair of modern lovers out on a weekend ramble. But they are a Victorian couple, and Hardy typically gives the history and geography of context. This good time shows its deep roots in a particular landscape and a social occasion, as the narrator points out the change made in the old thoroughfare from London to Land's End, which has been laid desolate by the coming of the railway. When Sue feels tired they find a shepherd who knows the times of trains. Like Shakespeare in Arden, Hardy does not romanticize his pastoral, and Jude's praise of the nice little rural cottage provokes the shepherd's mother's concern with the high price of thatch. The pastoral is earthed, by the trains, the road's history, and economic detail.

The cottage is a respite, like the whole day, not a total escape. Sue articulates the sense of holiday freedom, '"I rather like this," said Sue, while their entertainers were clearing away the dishes. "Outside all laws except gravitation and germination"' (Bk 3, Chap. 2). Jude disagrees, taxing her with being 'a product of civilisation', but she insists on a craving 'for the life of my infancy, and its freedom'. For one innocent day and night she gets it, but of course the chapter ends next morning with the late return, and the porter's grim face as he opens the gate, boundary and terminus. The good holiday has a beginning, a middle and an end. It chronicles common pleasures of friendship – plans, journey, visit to a stately home, paintings, country walk, supper, bed and breakfast, and good talk. Freedom comes not from wildness but from relaxed pleasures outside the routines and boundaries of work, institutional life and conventional codes. The three-page chapter is finely compressed and complete.

The next holiday is briefer. Nor is it quite so undisturbed. Soon after Sue's marriage to Phillotson, Jude pays her a visit on the day before Good Friday, and the occasion is a little like the spoiled or weary feast Thackeray devises so brilliantly, but there is a good time at the core. The visit begins badly with Jude getting one delayed letter of invitation and a second grudging one. Things look brighter when he arrives by train and climbs to Shaston, the 'world-forgotten' village inaccessible by rail. It is a 'breezy and inaccessible spot' where he hears young voices and sees girls in white pinafores and red dresses dancing along the Abbey paths. The omens are good, and while waiting for Sue he strums the hymn he admired but whose composer has turned out to be commonplace and mercenary. The piano playing gets even happier as Sue takes over with her skilled fingers and the playing is twice spontaneously interrupted as the loving friends grasp hands. Her playing seems 'divine', the unpremeditated touch is more erotic than anything else in the novel, and there are repeated signs and admissions of affinity, when she fondly wonders at Jude's visit to the composer – 'O you goose – to do just what I should have done!' and in the free mutuality of the touch, 'How funny!. . . . I wonder what we both did that for?' (Bk 4, Chap. 1).

Like the previous episode, this is an actual holiday, holy and secular, at Easter. Jude takes time off work, for a sharing of company and culture, music, tea and talk. The music itself is not erotic, but brings emotional stimulus and nostalgic intimacy, 'I learnt it before I left Melchester.' There is a small break with routine, as they have tea informally, not in her married home but the schoolroom, and again it is Sue who makes freedom explicit:

> 'Now we'll have some tea . . . Shall we have it here instead of in my house?. . . . Such houses are very well to visit, but not to live in – I feel crushed into the earth by the weight of so many previous lives there spent. In a new place like these schools there is only your own life to support.' (Bk 4, Chap. 1)

Shaston is a sympathetically raffish habitat for the play and relaxation. Its unconventional freedoms are detailed, and compounded by a bird image:

> the resting-place and headquarters of the proprietors of wandering vans, shows, shooting-galleries, and other itinerant concerns, whose business lay chiefly at fairs and markets. As strange wild birds are seen assembled on some lofty promontory, meditatively pausing for longer

flights . . . here . . . stood . . . the yellow and green
caravans bearing names not local . . . (Bk 4, Chap.1)

The habitat has no direct bearing on the tea-drinking,
but indirectly contributes to the prim but disturbing
occasion. Again, less than carnival, but warm with the
small liberties of holiday, and set in an appropriate place.

The third outing comes late in the novel, and it is
socially placed, as a public holiday for the Agricultural
show at Stoke-Barehills, served by the excursion train
bringing Arabella and her husband amongst the Londoners
on a day trip. The good times are explicitly recognized,
'That the twain were happy — between their times of
sadness — was indubitable'. Once more there is a small but
significant change: this sentence revises the Harper's serial
text, which reads 'It was possibly true that the twain were
happy — between their times of sadness', and the revision
makes the happy times definite.

On this outing Sue and Jude take Little Time with
them. The good time is a family treat, enclosing the
lovers' privacy, refracted at times through Arabella's
'sharpened vision', 'He's charmed by her as if she were
some fairy!' (Bk 5, Chap. 5). It is intimate close-up,
dramatized or freely and indirectly narrated, the viewpoint
constantly shifting, to intensify the delighted affinity at
the heart of the scene and register its flow and variety:
refreshment tent, demonstration of malting, cart-horse
shed, Art department, flower-show, band and cheapjack.
Arabella's purchase of the love potion keeps in touch with
the sleazy side of fairs and markets, so prominent in *The
Mayor of Casterbridge*, and perhaps recalls the rankness of
Spenser's bower.

The lovers's companionable happiness is set in a crowd.
Their own creativity is on show, ironically and plausibly,
in the model of Cardinal College, and they make the

exhibition an occasion 'which should combine exercise and amusement with instruction, at small expense'. An educated working-class couple taking their pleasure seriously, they wear their best, Sue in new summer clothes, Jude in his light grey holiday suit, and festive appearance is matched by shared pleasure: 'That complete mutual understanding, in which every glance and movement was as effectual as speech for conveying intelligence beween them, made them almost the two parts of a single whole'. Their closeness is physical too: they listen to music, '. . . deeply absorbed in their own lives, as translated into emotion by the military band', scrutinized by the veiled Arabella as they hold hands and stand 'close together so as to conceal, as they supposed, this tacit expression of their mutual responsiveness'.

Arabella takes and gives the deep jealous imprint of their union, and in the final episode of the scene, in the pavilion of flowers, she anticipates those critics who think Sue cold, but the bower of bliss proves her wrong. Sue is at her most sensuous and relaxed. She learns the names of the roses with her school-teacher's pedantic conscientiousness but feels she is in an enchanted palace and flushes like the pink roses 'she adored', in a total sensuous response, 'to the gay sights, the air, the music, and the excitement of a day's outing with Jude' which 'quickened her blood and made her eyes sparkle with vivacity'. When she longs to push her face into the roses, 'the dears', he 'playfully' gives 'her a little push, so that her nose went among the petals', teasing her, 'you baby'.

Once more, a rare scene where the lovers relax, have fun, share creativity and love the creativity in each other. It is a working-class, Victorian, bower of bliss, crucial in the problematic presentation of Sue. For a moment Hardy leaves behind the suggestions of her frigidity, and – perhaps intuitively – shows her relaxed into warmth, sensuousness and delighted touch. This scene offers a

brilliant perception that what has been suggested (by
Jude's words and her behaviour before they sleep
together) as her sexual coldness, is not a deep or perma-
nent condition. The bliss is presented, not dwelt on, but
its mutuality is plain: ' "Happy?" he murmured', and Sue
evades a direct answer, but not lightly or coldly, with
affectionate teasing jokes about improving her mind with
steam-ploughs, threshing machines and chaff-cutters. She
finally articulates, for the last time, a sense of freedom
from history and contingency, a defence of Hellenism, a
rejection of Christian ethic:

'I feel that we have returned to Greek joyousness, and
have blinded ourselves to sickness and sorrow, and have
forgotten what twenty-five centuries have taught the
race . . .'. (*loc. cit.*)

As when she made her earnest proposal to leave Phillotson, maddeningly peppered with quotations from John
Stuart Mill, Sue is the priggish schoolteacher even as she
proclaims pagan freedom. This is Hardy's truthfulness. He
knows we cannot escape the language of our culture even
while we dream of doing so. Here too the New Woman
Hardy was not aware of creating but did not deny when
told he had created her, is the imaginative spokesperson
for an impossible but life-supporting ideal of freedom. It
is the revelation of her sexual normality in this scene,
which makes her final Christian–masochistic return to a
loathed marriage-bed so horrifying. But this relapse is in
the future, and the only shadow on the happy scene is
Little Time's famous gloom, at its end: 'I should like the
flowers very very much, if I didn't keep on thinking
they'd all be withered in a few days!'.

It is a very good time, roses, teasing, touch and all,
with poetry and humour in the fond lovers and the
relaxed writing. The scene is affectionate, charming, sen-

suous and light-hearted, in spite of the shadow of Little Time and Arabella's love philtre. Again, too tame for carnival but abandoned enough for these hard-working repressed Victorian people at their provincial culture-feast. The popular culture of holiday is setting and symbol.

All these occasions emphasize happiness and its ordinariness. The pleasures of imagination are everyday stuff, attainable and unromantic. They are not wholly fantastic, but they show what might be kept and is lost. The sociology of Victorian holiday is matter-of-factly documented and made into a moderate sensuous poetry, a glimpse of freedom.

The good time is a part which stands for that unconditional whole, but has its own pragmatic reality, showing the possibilities of untragic life with human beings propped and stayed for a span by nature, culture and relationship. Hardy's network of internal narrative and figurations, which draws attention to the form and theme of his large construction, joins with this handful of actualized and unmediated good times. They enlarge and modify his tragic selection, placing it as individual impression and unsettling or confounding any appearance of dogmatic, authoritarian form. In order to read Hardy properly we must read him closely.

CHAPTER FOUR

Portraits of the Artist in the Poems

Tess is Hardy's best complete portrait of creativity. Whatever his intention in making such an image, and it is unlikely that it was wholly conscious, the act of imagining forceful imagination is integral to the novel as a whole, to its portrait of a woman and her determining conditions. The novel is about more than imagination, and it assimilates the subject of creativity to the tragic story with great subtlety. The subject is deeply plumbed. We have only to compare the interiorization of shaping and speaking in the character of Tess with explicit remarks about art in the earlier novels to recognize the achieved power of Hardy's indirection. To repeat, in his prose fiction he imagines creativity most profoundly when his mind is not on the making of art but on some other subject, when artistic self-consciousness is relaxed and off-duty.

This is not true of his poetry, where the professional artists are much more passionately presented, because the genre is one in which the writer's emotions are freer and more intensely concentrated. Whether Hardy is working with professional artists like the inventor or discoverer of the Perpendicular Style, the anonymous architect-hero of 'The Abbey Mason', or the first-person writer of an unspecified text as in 'An August Midnight' and 'On a Midsummer Eve', the poetry is thoroughly engaged with artistic creativity. A number of poems, like the rustic choruses in the novels, but passionately, particularize and impersonate the imagination of the gifted amateur, like his rapt story-telling grandmother's in 'One We Knew', and even more implicitly and impersonally reveal the creativity of everyday life, that of a brooding lover on a railway journey or someone listening to a winter thrush.

The short lyrics and some of the narrative poems concentrate on emotion, freed from the complicated histories and psychologies of prose fiction to articulate affective experience without history or explanation. The act of emotional generation is revealed and self-analysing. We should remember that Hardy began and ended with poetry. Fine though his novels are – and I do not think there is anything gained by lengthy comparative judgements of the two genres – they are willed, commercial, breadwinning work compared with the less lucrative poems which at first could not command publication, let alone royalties. His novels generate and are generated by the passions but for long stretches in any long narrative, as genius labours, relaxes, idles or deliberates in its prose exercise, intensities are not sustainable. In the Preface to *Wessex Poems* Hardy declares that his verse was written for himself: it was 'the more individual part' of his 'literary fruitage', because in it 'nothing interfered with the writer's freedom in form or in content'. In poetry Hardy can feel his subjects without thinking of pleasing or censoring, without naming, defining or completing. A novel is a huge commitment, a poem a small one, to be offered or kept or thrown away without a burden of commercial anxiety. Poets can please themselves – more – in any individual poem, can be freer, less inhibited, more intuitive, more open, and let the unconscious play a larger part. The poet can be mere fragment or all indirection.

Of course Hardy the poet can be direct and developmental too. But even his occasional poems about art and literature, the formal or informal Homages to other artists – usually writers or composers – are never mere compliments but are one way and another genuinely attentive to the subject. Admired writers like Shakespeare, Tennyson,[1] and Shelley are not so often drawn into the novels' fabric of feeling as fully or pointedly as they are in the poems, which contemplate the subject feelingly and hardly ever simply incorporate allusion and quotation as the novels frequently do.

Some of Hardy's verses about other poets or musicians are low-key pieces but they nearly all pay their homage to ancestors and contemporaries thoughtfully and sensitively.

One stanza of 'An Ancient to Ancients' economically revises the melancholy detail of Tennyson's 'Mariana' to lament Tennyson's heyday and contemporary decadence. Hardy follows Tennyson in assonance, alliteration, compounds, octosyllabics, refrain (but uses a short line instead of quatrain), and details of building, but his spider is new, having obviously eaten Tennyson's blue fly in the pane. Best homage of all, the imitation invites the reader to remember or re-read:

> The bower we shrined to Tennyson,
> > Gentlemen,
> Is roof-wrecked; damps there drip upon
> Sagged seats, the creeper-nails are rust,
> The spider is sole denizen;
> Even she who voiced those rhymes is dust,
> > Gentlemen!

Less close in imitation, 'George Meredith. 1828–1909' recalls Meredith's trenchancy, exuberance, kindness and obscurity, in faithful images of morning, wings and music, uses mimetic diction like 'vaporous vitiate', intimately remembers – no need to name – 'his green hill', and praises the radical fervent sincerity so congenial to Hardy in spite of its optimism. He and Meredith shared enemies in conservatism, Christianity and cant:

He was of those whose wit can shake
And riddle to the very core
The counterfeits that Time will break. . . .

Swinburne was another congenial spirit and 'A Singer Asleep' is a bold rhapsodic pastiche, its apt polysyllabic effusiveness, but not its elaborate stanza, far from Hardy's manner, and the vivid joke about Victorian family values in character for both poets, 'It was as though a garland of red roses / Had fallen about the hood of some smug nun'.

Hardy's musical mimicry is clever in remembering Swinburne, and in poems about music, like 'Barthélémon At Vauxhall' the imitation of Barthélémon's and Bishop Ken's hymn, which cleverly incorporates rather than imitates the original line. There is the virtuoso piece, 'Lines to a Movement in Mozart's E-Flat Symphony', where Hardy anticipates the fluid musicalization of language by Gerard Manley Hopkins and James Joyce, imitating the music and rhapsodizing about love at the same time: 'such surging, swaying, sighing, swelling, shrinking' and 'such ratheness, rareness, ripeness, richness, rashness'.

Hardy wrote several poems about Keats. 'At a House in Hampstead' discusses the places of Keats's memorial rather than Keats but firmly attaches itself to the poetry as it evokes the absence of nightingales and re-uses one of Keats's best adjectives, 'never a nightingale pours one / Full-throated sound?' 'The Selfsame Song' is an oblique homage where we may not even notice the Keatsian allusion, since the overt subject is the survival of a bird's song and the death of friends 'who heard / That song with me'. The short poem works very indirectly, by a reversal of a key subject, recalling the Ode by apostrophizing a bird's immortal song, then revising, the Keatsian trope, 'Thou wert not born for death, immortal bird', and appropriating the image for his own new lament: 'But it's not the selfsame bird. – / No, perished to dust is he'. He praises by not naming, and even argues a little with the poet and his poem, as he does more centrally and elaborately in 'Shelley's Skylark'. But his most powerful homage to Keats, 'At Lulworth Cove a Century Back', also a poem of indirection, is most skilfully constructed to tease and explain in ways appropriate to the poet's life, and death.

The identification of Keats is deferred in the dialogue between an ignorant man tired by walking in the dark, and the urgent ironic voice of all-knowing Time, which eventually reveals that the man in Lulworth a century ago was on his way 'to Rome – to death, despair', but also that in another century, 'the world will follow him there'. The slow development of the poem is perfect for the slow growth of Keats's reputation.

Its strength also depends on the refusal to name, in the knowledge that the reader never needs to have the name spelt out, though the speed of understanding will vary. The puzzle is set, and elucidated step by step, by irony, the repeated imperatives, '*You see that man?*', and the allusion to the bright star, 'He looks up at a star, as many do'. (This was chosen because Hardy thought the sonnet 'Bright star! Would I were steadfast as thou art' was written at Lulworth, though Keats only made a fair copy of it there.) Keats, like Shelley, was often in Hardy's mind, and he creates a dialogue which brims with admiration and sympathy, for the man's life as well as his poetry, but solves the problem of how to praise warmly and reticently.

The poem shows, metonymically, how a name is made, concluding only after Time has insisted three times that the innocent speaker on whom Time has 'placed his finger' – a great image for the poem's tender piercing insight – should look at the 'thin' and 'idling' youth. The subtext of fatal illness is repressed until the revelation,

which still refrains from naming Keats. It has it both ways:
the reader who makes the right inference or guesses at the
beginning, can share Time's irony; the reader who has to
wait till the end will be surprised and perhaps guilty; and
both will prove the poem's point about the irony of
reputation. Time's last stanza wonderfully affirms the
unnamed poet. Hardy's metrical skill shows itself particularly in the heavy stress on 'world', after the two light
stresses, and in an extra-syllabic line:

'Good. That man goes to Rome – to death, despair;
And no one notes him now but you and I:
A hundred years, and the world will follow him there,
And bend with reverence where his ashes lie.'

'Shelley's Skylark' also sends us back to remember or
re-read, as poetic homage should, and in this case very
pointedly:

Somewhere afield here something lies
In Earth's oblivious eyeless trust
That moved a poet to prophecies –
A pinch of unseen, unguarded dust.

The dust of the lark that Shelley heard,
And made immortal through times to be; –

After this disarming start, it goes on to praise and judge
the dead poet by radically re-imagining his poem, in an
affectionate backhanded compliment which shows the
new poet's saturation in the old poet's work. It is cleverly
dialogic, its critique deeply subtextualized. It disingenu-
ously assumes an ingenuous romantic praise, claiming that
the lark made immortal by the poem really lived, 'like
another bird, / And knew not its immortality'. Shelley's
'bird' that 'never wert' is never the same again after

Hardy's insistently accurate 'Lived its meek life; then, one day, fell- / A little ball of feather and bone . . .'. The bird's life and death are precisely and affectionately imagined; exactly as they are not imagined by Shelley, whose method is abstraction, whose conclusion is romantic, and whose lark is heroic not meek, immortal not mortal, ideal not physical. Hardy's poem is praise with a core of dissent, a materialization in his own manner which dares to argue with Shelley's ideal, reviving it as it revises. It is also, like the much simpler 'At a House in Hampstead', sharply aware of itself as a memorial. This is not simply because it revises the abstraction in the source-poem, but because it presents an alternative candidate for memorial, in the dead bird whose remains and grave are 'unguarded' and unremembered, unlike the remains and tombs of dead poets.

Hardy also dares, in a brilliantly discreet way, to revise Shakespeare, not in the homage-poem 'Shakespeare', with its fine image for power and strangeness, 'the strange bright fowl amongst the barnhens', but in his love poem 'The End of the Episode'. In it he uses indirection and anonymity again, as he revises for his own purposes one of Shakespeare's most quoted lines. It is *A Midsummer Night's Dream*'s 'The path of true love never did run smooth', so familiar that it is sometimes often spoken for a laugh in modern productions. It is pondered, revised, deepened, matched and unmistakably recalled in Hardy's new-imagined stoically endured hurt. Hardy's craft of preparation is at work in the last stanza, where two tight and tightly punctuated lines, mostly monosyllable, prepare for the powerful reminiscent outburst with its single telling long word:

> Ache deep; but make no moans:
> Smile out; but stilly suffer:
> The paths of love are rougher
> Than thoroughfares of stones.

Moving from Hardy's real artists to fictitious ones, we find an imaginatively detailed tribute in 'The Abbey Mason', whose subject is congenial to Hardy, specifically, because it is architectural, and more generally, because it emphasizes collaboration between art and nature. It argues that informed and practised art must be open to intuition, chance and immediacy. (One of many artists' anticipations of Edward de Bono's idea of lateral thinking.)

The poem is by far the best thing he wrote about his first profession, which the early novels deal with laboriously and pedantically. The idea is set out in the poem naïvely and didactically, but the manner is appropriate for its mediaeval setting and simple Christian characters. The Abbey Mason feels guilty about getting his aesthetic solution from nature: having left his chalked plan out in the cold, he finds the structural problem of joining upper and lower curves in an arch accidentally solved by the pattern made by frozen rainmarks on the drawing-board. Anxious about his own apparently small and passive part in this creative collaboration, he is reassured by his superior that the result is neither culpable nor unprecedented, 'art can but transmute; / Invention is not absolute'. In any case, he has begun and ended the pattern himself, adding his own 'accessory cusping marks'.

Hardy always loves the technical terms of architecture and in this story the details of craft come into their own, with none of the redundant information which sometimes flaws description in the novels. The passion of the craftsman is tenderly rendered, and the poem creates character, tells a story, and draws its aesthetic moral with a clear simplicity. It is the kind of thing he sometimes tries for in vain in the novels and brings off effectively in this short poem, as he affectionately imagines the practical problems and the high formal vision of Gothic sublimity, dramatically, and from the inside of a mind. It is a poem you cannot imagine being written by someone who was not both an architect and a poet.

One of his best portraits of an artist, 'The Chapel Organist' (discussed more fully in Chapter Seven) is about a passion for art and about physical performance, showing the sexuality of the musician as both inseparable from her music-making, and in conflict with it. What some of his heroes or heroines do for love – Giles and Tess – this passionate heroine does for art, choosing not only to prefer it to sexual pleasure but to die rather than live without it. Of course Hardy is doing other things as well, like ridiculing and criticizing the ignorant repressed chapel elders who can not tolerate – or tolerate for mercenary reasons – the organist's private life, and he is critical of their ignorance. They do not know why they enjoy the sensuality of the music and they think art and life can be separated. Hardy daringly invokes a composite Muse to refute them: the organist's contralto voice, her hands, her throat, her bosom, her sexual experience and her imagination make her music, and her story, in ways she knows and others she does not know.

That collaboration between the conscious and unconscious mind, choice and chance, art and nature, is a preoccupation of the poems, and central to the poetry about imagination. It is the theme of a pair of twinned love-poems, 'Why Did I Sketch?' and 'The Figure in the Scene', inspired by one of Hardy's own drawings which survives in the Dorset County Library. Each poem is about someone making an image of the beloved which survives to recall the past, the first in a simply contemplated painful memorial, the other in a passionate analysis of creativity, love and memory.

'The Figure in the Scene' builds an image, as it tells a story, of the layering enterprise of imagination, but as the artist accrues details it obscures, instead of bringing out, the picture being drawn. There is a darkening of the model, first by rain staining and spotting of the canvas, then by the bars of falling rain, which get into the picture, then by the hood the woman wears against weather, and lastly by distance and time. The process of physical reduction and darkening allows the poet to make his abstraction and end with an image of power, 'a rainy Form' which has become 'the genius still of the spot' because the human has been dematerialized and sublimed into a more than individual figure, and can be transformed into memorial. With that word genius, the woman is apotheosized, as Milton's dead poet is made genius of the shore in 'Lycidas'.

Hardy's matter-of-factness characteristically adds another veiling layer, in the preservation of the particular origin from posterity's 'curious quizzings'. The poet is doing with the poem what the artist in the poem did with the picture, daring the reader by making an apt prophetic joke about biographical curiosity. He is also demonstrating the transformations of art. Great and little subjects are held in tension, with Hardy's high seriousness, light touch, his wry humour, the engaging blend. It is a poem about imagination, but also a poem about sketching a woman in a rain-hat on rainspotted canvas or paper. The poem is particular and abstract, about love and art. It is also about its own generation, showing how poetry abstracts the particular, and memory preserves it, how intention is modified by accident, adapting inner drive, original impulse and raw material to meet the immediate and the unpremeditated, and in the end doing better than the artist dreamed. The painter is rewarded for being an opportunist as well as passionate lover. And it is all done in two nine-line stanzas of simple words. It is now a commonplace to say that poems are about themselves but this poem becomes reflexive by a miniaturization of another genre. Comparing it with its twin poem – more painful and much simpler – shows how the same source can produce poems that are very different, emotionally, structurally and intellectually.

Hardy often writes about writing, sometimes directly, as in 'The Dead Man Walking', a forcefully condensed poem which contains one eloquent local image of creativity. Unusual amongst his elegies, it describes the silent inch-by-inch death of man and poet:

> They hail me as one living,
>   But don't they know
> That I have died of late years
>   Untombed although?

This is Hardy's modestly ironic contribution to the poetry of failed inspiration, and though it scarcely competes with masterpieces like 'Dejection: An Ode' and 'The Circus Animals' Desertion', the dense reflexive lines of one stanza effectively clench form and feeling together in sound and image, as the 'pulseless' man who has outlived his life and art tersely recalls his passions:

> – A Troubadour-youth I rambled
>   With Life for lyre,
> The beats of being raging
>   In me like fire.

The poetry is about itself in more ways than one. The tidy simple bald sound and images which surround this single animated stanza, are right for the mechanical motion – mere 'walking' – which is all he can manage now. Hardy's self-reflection in that stanza is not merely self-absorbed as it recalls old excitements of art and the larger life outside art, invoking them explicitly, though figuratively, in rekindled heat and revived beat, and formally, in the rhyme and rhythmically stressed vowel and consonant pattern. The poem dramatizes while it narrates and describes the subject, and the identification of past fervours of life and art is neatly, though bitterly, completed by the echoing consonants and vowels in 'Life for lyre', 'beats of being' and 'like fire'. The beat is figurative and literal, and the musical pattern binds, distinguishes, and finally demonstrates the action of metaphor as it shuttles between the two meanings, the beat of the poem and the heart. It is the stanza which proves that the heart, like the verse, is still beating, in order to argue its death. After its brief warm vigorous interval the deadening is resumed, the man 'iced'. Hardy finds his own solution to the problem of writing poetry about not being able to write.

A simpler poem about poetry is 'Her Definition', not one of his best poems about creativity but interestingly imitating George Herbert's poetry against rhetoric, which uses simple or bare words to reject decoration or formality, in reflexive demonstration of plain language. Hardy adapts Herbert's devotional austerity for a love-praise: he places the phrase 'That maiden mine' in the sixth line of the sonnet, as the preferred 'sole speech' which shows that the praise of love must choose plainness, after five lines describing his search for appropriately 'full-featured terms', a witty body-metaphor, the minimalist example, 'That maiden mine,' and the critical conclusion. He explains what is happening, 'the indefinite phrase could yet define', but the poem shows as well as tells, in a complex form of *occupatio*. Admitting that the poet does not need ornament, its sestet is entirely taken up by an elaborate, Herbert-like conceit, figuring a simple vehicle for a costly tenor. In its way it is an inappropriate 'outfiguring' of the beloved and given pride of place after the sonnet's turn, in conclusion:

As common chests encasing wares of price
Are borne with tenderness through halls of state,

For what they cover, so the poor device
Of homely wording I could tolerate,
Knowing its unadornment held as freight
The sweetest image outside Paradise.

Just occasionally, Hardy writes a poem, like this, which
may seem naïve or sophisticated: perhaps the left hand
does not quite know what the right is doing; perhaps he
is pondering decorum, figuration, and the relation of
tenor to vehicle, letting the poem insist on 'unadornment'
but by constructing an adornment in the conceit of the
chests borne through halls of state. Does the poem fall on
its face or is it amused by its own slyness?

This kind of analysis and introspection is rare in Hardy,
who prefers a poetry of a more performative and less
ingenious reflexivity, like 'An August Midnight', where
the process of making is a covert subject. This is not in
any obvious way a poem about art, but at first reading
about an encounter of a human being with non-human
nature. Creativity emerges from sub-text to become
revealed text.

The title and the first line set the scene and direct the
entry, 'A shaded lamp and a waving blind', and begin the
gentle, spare story-telling, about the soft arrival and
behaviour of four small insects. The poem favours nuance
and indirection. It specifies light and hints at heat in the
image of the open window, so we know why and how
the creatures come, and the 'beat of a clock from a distant
floor' tells how the writer tells the time. Details of
appearance suggest the costume of melodrama but introduce a quiet minimal action:

On this scene enter – winged, horned, and spined –
A longlegs, a moth, and a dumbledore;
While 'mid my page there idly stands
A sleepy fly, that rubs its hands . . .

The guests arrive to revise the text, as we gather when 'the page' reveals the act of writing, fresh writing, 'My guests besmear my new-penned line'. Their arrival, so common and slight an event as to guarantee authenticity, is the occasion for another unassuming but ambitious poem about itself, another demonstration of writing to the moment. This is too polished to be called unpremeditated art, but it is about the unpremeditated moment, and in part improvised from the given and the accidental.

The poet combines pleasure in the event with a companionable feeling for the creatures, again with the lightest of light touches. Just as he modestly revises his sense that they are 'God's humblest', so he keeps his writing muted, and the hospitable 'Thus meet we five', offers a quiet welcome to the creatures that complete the poem, and are as necessary to it as the human moving pen and brain and heart.

In this modest poem about writing – as well as animals – as in the poems about sketching in the open air, the artist is caught in the act of composition. In 'The Monument-Maker' the artist, a monumental mason and sculptor, has just finished an ambitious and weighty project, and declares that it has turned out exactly as planned.

> I chiselled her monument
>   To my mind's content,
> Took it to the church by night,
> When her planet was at its height,
> And set it where I had figured the place in the daytime.
>   Having niched it there
> I stepped back, cheered, and thought its outlines fair,
>   And its marbles rare.

He looks on his work and finds it good, like God and the Abbey Mason, but his complacency, at the beginning of the poem, issues a dangerous invitation to the commemorated dead. The Abbey Mason laughed with pleasure but in this poem the one who laughs is the dead woman looking critically at her marble memorial. Setting up the image and feeling he had her 'niched' – a good metonymy – with her planet at its height, was rash magic, and no wonder her unsolicited ghost looks over the sculptor's shoulder instead of staying still under his gaze, gazes herself, and rejects his art:

> 'It spells not me!' she said:
> 'Tells nothing about my beauty, wit, or gay
> time
> With all those, quick and dead,
> Of high or lowlihead,
> That hovered near,
> Including you, who carve there your devotion;
> But you felt none, my dear!'

After this strong interchange, the third stanza seems a feeble ending, on a first reading. The woman vanishes after rejecting the monument and having her say, the man weeps because he has not been truly known or prized by her, and his monument is scorned. The 'scorned' is qualified, by markers of hope, 'scorned, almost,' and 'Yet I hoped not quite, in her very innermost!' and with lame hope the poem limps off. The layerings are not strengthenings but weakenings, and the ending tails away honestly, having been taken over and enfeebled by the ghost, in an act of creative destruction. The act is as good as breaking the inadequate monument, since the poem contains the monument, and is the monument, just as the monument is the poem's metonym and the monument-maker the poet's alias.

This revengefully triumphant woman-ghost with her counter-text is like the other ghost in an earlier poem 'The Haunter', one of the 1913 elegies, also a self-deconstructing lyric where the poet – or rather his poem – is aware that he is appropriating the voice of another human being, Emma, his once-loved, estranged, dead wife. Hardy's imagining of imagination is no simple artistic self-consciousness, but involves such abrasive projections. In 'The Haunter' the dead woman finally offers faithful love and solicitude to the bereaved speaker but hints – and it is the quietest hinting – that the ghost's hovering repeats a hovering in life, which has different implications, of timidity, doubt, distance and alienation. The word 'hover' is used in 'The Monument-Maker' to describe the admirers who are held at a distance, and asserts her confidence and power, and this later poem, dated 1916, is a revision of the more ambivalent poem written about three years before, extracting and articulating the sense of elegiac and memorial appropriation. The earlier poem offered goodwill, and only an undercurrent of reproach, though its claim 'What a good haunter am I' turns out true in a sense the poet had perhaps not grasped in the months just after Emma's death, when he was imagining her instrumentally rather than objectively.

Emma is allowed on this later occasion to be oppositional, to reject the elegeic mode, to take a grim hand in the poem, and turn round its intent. The simple obituary remembrances of Mother Cuxsom and Marty South, spoken as ritual acts, do not imagine the dead's response, but the bereaved Hardy often did. Hardy's mood obviously oscillated, as he wrote out of the common attempt to re-imagine the past, romantically settling things to his satisfaction in 'After a Journey' and 'At Castle Boterel', at other times seeing the redundancy and the wishfulfilment of remorse and reunion. The unromantic elegies invent the reproachful ghost to counter the reconciled ghost who was even imagined as accepting the assurance in 'After a Journey', that the lover is 'the same' as he was when their day was fair.

Some of these extraordinary poems are written against
the elegiac simplification of others, in a way unprecedented, as far as I know, in elegy, though there may be
something like it in the twists and turns of *In Memoriam*.
By imagining the point of view of the elegiac object,
Hardy turns it into artist and authority, gives it a first
person's voice and power to undermine his poetic authority. This is not only paying proper attention to another
human being (or ghost) and refusing to imagine for
someone else (hard to do in life or poetry) but showing
an artist's pragmatism, giving up expectation to meet the
unpredictable or intransigent. He incorporates into the
poem a sense of the limits of egocentric imagination,
showing the artist at work in the act of ordering or
unifying experience but resisted by disorderly rebellious
life. His artist is surprised in a way neither easy nor
pleasurable, but unselving, imagining as his best self. It is
all very well to see that imagination creates dynamically,
and generates forms of feeling in the act of creation but it
is a less comfortable experience to generate contradiction
which checks and undermines us.

That lame uncertainty which fades out 'The Monument-Maker' is perfect for the experience of being dis-
concerted, losing solace and authority and confidence.
The appropriation of the dead is deconstructed, and with
it the unity and solace of elegy. On this occasion artistic
self-consciousness is an enlargement, a reaching-out of
imagination, a change of heart.

Another poem about imaginative construction in which
the ghost of a past refuses burial but seizes the pen more
benignly, is the bewitching lyric 'On a Midsummer Eve'.
Here the rituals of midsummer magic – raising visions
through natural magic of moon, plants, water – become
and join images of art, while the images of art join to
become midsummer magic. Artistic creation may be a
ritual, involving the following of traditional practice and

form in a way which is individual and obedient. Here the poet, for whom number is important, uses the magic number three, repeating three ceremonies of passive initiation which use art to solicit nature. Relaxation, ignorance, surprise and fear are repeated and varied. The arts are varied too: the first stanza is musical, the player improvising with a pipe made from the hollow parsley (cow-parsley) stalk:

> I idly cut a parsley stalk,
> And blew therein towards the moon;
> I had not thought what ghosts would walk
> With shivering footsteps to my tune.

Next comes the making of a visual image, figuration behind the turned back, or reflection?:

> I went, and knelt, and scooped my hand
> As if to drink, into the brook,
> And a faint figure seemed to stand
> Above me, with the bygone look.

Then comes unconscious art in improvised rhyme:

> I lipped rough rhymes of chance, not choice,
> I thought not what my words might be;
> There came into my ear a voice
> That turned a tenderer verse for me.

The artist is idling not designing, using the materials that are at hand, a plant, the brook, his hand, unsought rhymes. His art collaborates with nature. Each act has something magical about it, belonging to midsummer. The flute-song is blown towards the moon, dominant as 'her planet' is in 'The Monument-Maker', and ghosts walk – or may walk, because the haunting is at first kept

delicately provisional. The usual tentative verb is present
as the ghost imagined by not being imagined 'seemed' to
appear, perhaps in the brook's mirror, and the voice at
the end may be external or internal, 'came into my ear'.
By the end the double magic of midsummer ritual and
artistic fiats have joined in a metaphor not only for art
and magic but also for love and memory. The ghosts are
raised by invitation as they must be in magic, and unconsciously as they must be in art, involuntary memory, and
love, which cannot be willed.

It is all process, like art and memory, the haunting
slowly becoming more marked, though always indefinite,
even as the completions are welcomed as love. It begins
with a negative, not thinking, and the ghost's footsteps
are shivering because faint, wavery, unstable, perhaps
timid and cold even at midsummer, mere tentative fig-
ments. The ghost becomes more definite as it is identified
in the singular, still only a seeming, only a reflection, and
behind, not face-to-face, but visualized, as a 'bygone
look'. 'Bygone look' is both a familiar past and an old-
fashioned costume.

When the voice is heard in tender rhyme, we know it
is all one haunting, image-reinforcing image and revealed
as the haunting of love when the action within the poem
comes to coincide with the poem's own rhyme and turn.
Reflexivity is compounded; the poem which began with
the innocent creative fiat ends in clarification. Perhaps the
reader is less innocent than the speaker, being alerted by
the title. Once more a ghost completes the poem. The
composite Muse, a beloved from the past as well as a
Muse, takes us from passivity to activity, but uncertainly
and suggestively, as a ghost should. Art has been ritual, in
another of Hardy's short poems with a long imaginative
trajectory.

Another poem about creative haunting is 'In Front of
the Landscape', where many ghosts gather in a powerful

group haunting. The haunted is not that of a maker but a visionary, at least from one point of view. The title announces a process of dislocation, in which the speaker begins with an image of obstruction, as he moves on foot through a tide, hampered by water and mist. The tide is made 'of visions' playing on the obscured scenes of a real place, 'the customed landscape'. This landscape has been defamiliarized. When Coleridge, in the *Biographia Literaria*, talks of the transformation of quotidian dullness by Wordsworth's poetry or his own, it is to see it as valuable but the speaker here hankers after the ordinary life, which is being traumatically threatened. What has been solid is – seemingly – dissolved, 'Seemed but a ghost-like gauze, and no substantial / Meadow or mound'.

The speaker is not entirely passive, and his voice takes some responsibility for the unwilled visions or 're-crea-tions' which 'killed the daytime'. Suddenly the insubstan-tial is given substance, and face:

> O they were speechful faces, gazing insistent,
> > Some as with smiles,
> Some as with slow-born tears that brinily trundled
> > Over the wrecked
> Cheeks that were fair in their flush-time . . .

Once again the ghosts are unwanted. The chief haunter is 'the one of the broad brow', and the haunting is by 'the bygone.' There is an image of seascape, the experience of physical ecstasy, lovers called 'two friends', perhaps in recall of Tristram and Iseult, famously called friends, their 'hoary' and 'gnawed' headland, and 'the fringe of an ecstasy / Scantly descried'. These ghosts are reproachful but also truly dead, and belief in the supernatural is kept at bay by the wary modifiers, 'as with', and 'as they were ghosts'. The obscured vision is a special revenge for the seer's blindness and neglect when they were alive, and the haunting, like most of Hardy's hauntings, is psychologically explicable:

> Much had I slighted, caring not for their purport,
> Seeing behind
> Things more coveted, . . .

At the end there is another admission of responsibility: though the poem is imprinted with a sense of involuntary pressure and possession, there is also the medium of the artist's imagination, 'the intenser / Stare of the mind' on which the ghosts are screened, to show 'with fuller translation than rested upon them / As living kind'. This poem creates an unusual − perhaps unique − tension between the receiving mind and the figuration, which makes it fascinating both as the psychology of remorse and as a ghost-story.

As in the midsummer poem, the conclusion for the seer is the conclusion for the reader: both are shocked by death. The speaker is shocked by the frightening external story, the reductive report of 'the tongues of the passing people' and the reader recognizes the insubstantiality, solidity, reverie and recall:

> 'Ah − whose is this dull form that perambulates, seeing
> nought
> Round him that looms
> Whithersoever his footsteps turn in his farings,
> Save a few tombs?'

We feel the terrible physicality and the psychic remoteness of the dead, in the phrase 'clay cadavers'. The outside view sees only a dull man, because the action has all been in the mind, and that is what haunting is. The long lines with polysyllabic diction and many feminine rhymes per-

ambulate retardingly and portentously through the pan-
orama, giving a sense of resistance and slow process, but
at last the phantasmagoria come to an abrupt end in the
last line's four monosyllables, where the haunted imagination moves into the commonsense broad daylight view
of things, 'Save a few tombs?' That question-mark may
take us back again to the beginning, as good conclusions
often do. This is Hardy's most dynamic and particularized
poem about the submission to the past, making us feel
from inside and outside the long trajectory of a self-
sickened obsessed imaginative remorse which knows its
own futility.

Hardy masters the underminings of seeming, making
them into a special trope of provisionality. He uses this
movingly when he imagines communicating with the
dead and the past, which can only be imagined and not
definitely known. However, it does not represent only
frustration but can summon its opposite, the sense of
communion. This very different form of scrupulous hesitation creates 'The Darkling Thrush', which is like 'An
August Midnight' in pulling back from anthropocentric
condescension. Once more Hardy writes about listening
to a bird's song, and the articulation of joy and profit
admits the fallaciousness of the pathetic fallacy. The listener is in need of comfort as he endures the wintry *fin de
siècle* in depression, and perhaps – though the poem does
not say so – old age: 'The land's sharp features seemed to
be / The Century's corpse', and 'every spirit upon earth
/ Seemed featureless as I'. Solace comes as an entry for
imagination, suddenly opened by the scrawny bird's soul-
flinging song of 'Joy illimited':

> That I could think there trembled through
>   His happy good-night air
> Some blessed Hope, whereof he knew
>   And I was unaware.

Here Hardy can allows himself to imagine a romantic unity of being by insisting that the idea is not believed but merely entertained. There is a similar fruitful interplay beween intellectual honesty and imaginative hope in 'The Last Chrysanthemum' which comes just before 'The Darkling Thrush' in *Poems of the Past and Present*. After imagining the flower's consciousness of summer's 'fervid call' and speculating about the reasons for its delayed appearance the speaker ends with the admission of fantasy but adds one further daring speculation, one of his most delicate articulations of belief. He figures the incorrigibility of faiths:

> — I talk as if the thing were born
> With sense to work its mind;
> Yet it is but one mask of many worn
> By the Great Face behind.

The sliding qualifications of the poem, leading to the final image of mask and face, make this a vision of the agnostic imagination at its most reverent and awed. It acknowledges mysteries, but we must not be tempted into seeing it as a statement of belief in the supernatural. 'I talk as if' is an exact description of what Hardy is doing in this poetry, which knows that it imagines, going so far but no farther.

CHAPTER FIVE

Arts of Conversation

Conversation in everyday life is dramatic and narrative. Its structures may not have been formally discussed until this century but its aesthetics, psychology and politics have always been observed and recreated by dramatic and narrative artists writing imaginary conversations as they invent and inquire. Their record is not usually explicit or taxonomic but it is clearly present in models of language and form intent on local literary functions and not analytically ambitious.

Conversation as an art is obviously imitated and practised in theatrical forms, in some more conspicuously than in others, for instance Congreve, Wilde, Noel Coward and Harold Pinter; and in prose fiction too, again very conspicuously in certain writers, for instance Jane Austen, Thomas Love Peacock, I. Compton Burnett, Henry James and Aldous Huxley. All these are specialists in conversation, loving the display and dialectic of good talk, inventing conversations which are like brilliant sustained rallies in tennis, showing off but also implicitly providing social, psychic and linguistic self-analysis.

And of course many novelists use and vary conversation brilliantly but less flamboyantly and concentratedly, for instance, Charlotte Brontë, George Eliot and Hardy.

Each artist practises an individual art of dialogue, and though it is certainly not his only conversational achievement, central in Hardy is his choric story-telling. We remember the great narrative setpieces of *Under the Greenwood Tree*, *The Woodlanders* and *The Return of the Native*, whose eloquent rustics present the jostle and competition

of anecdote, reminiscence and discussion in ways which
are historically and comically rich, but highlight the
exchange of experience in ways that are subtly self-
judging and self-analysing. Almost any example would
do, from the anecdotal party-chat at the tranter's house in
Under the Greenwood Tree to the reminiscences led by
Timothy Fairway in *The Return of the Native*.

Conversation has many functions, in art and life. In *The
Trumpet in the Dust* Constance Holme, a novelist good
enough to resemble Hardy and never imitate him, called
it the art form of the poor. It is not only the art of the
poor, though she needed to put it like that in her novel,
to emphasize a social need and fulfilment. Conversation is
in several senses a generative model, and the virtuoso
storytelling of Fairway and his supporting chorus is less
illustrative than some less comically brilliant, more evenhanded exchanges. Hardy was a great admirer and creator
of the virtuoso teller but he also loved to invent dialogue
which is a genuine sharing, a duet, a mutual inspiration
and prompting.

He had a fine ear for talk, in its way, or in its field, as
sharp and delicate as Jane Austen's. Like her he could
register a social situation, make comedy, differentiate
character, and reveal something about the form and flow
of talk, all at the same time. There is a delightful exchange
in *The Trumpet Major* which does all these things, providing a model of small talk and showing Hardy's ear for the
'made' conversation. He liked to create occasional bad
examples, like Thomas Leaf's stories, and the conversation
between Mrs Garland and Matilda is a good bad conversation, jerky, forced, self-conscious, never easing to
develop into dynamic exchange. The obverse of the
smooth flow of badinage in Wilde or I. Compton-Burnett
is this stiff, awkward and jerky artifice of self-conscious
cue-talking between these polite woman – two speakers,
with Ann as a silent third whose embarrassment we infer –

forced to make conversation. It is a gem, a self-analysing
social model and a good comic scene with a streak of wild
zany humour rare in Hardy. The exaggeration of the
model goes along with the making of character, as we
observe the social and psychological contrast between the
superior knowledge and commonsense of Mrs Garland,
and the floundering efforts of Matilda Johnson, a sympathetic fish-out-of-water camp-follower acting the fine lady
and trying to make it as Bob's affianced. Hardy did not
need to recall the conversation in *Mansfield Park* between
Fanny Price and Mary Crawford about wind and weather,
but this dialogue is a low-life version of it.

After an introductory generalization by the narrator,
the conversation begins economically with a first line
from an undesignated speaker; Hardy starts with Matilda
but the talk is kept rational by the senior lady Mrs
Garland, who is being nice to the visitor and finding it –
like her visitor – heavy going:

> But conversation, as such, was naturally at first of a
> nervous, tentative kind, in which, as in the works of
> some hazy poets, the sense was considerably led by the
> sound.
>
> 'You get the sea-breezes here, no doubt?'
> 'Oh yes, dear; when the wind is that way.'
> 'Do you like windy weather?'
> 'Yes; though not now, for it blows down the young
> apples.'
> 'Apples are plentiful, it seems. You country-folk call
> St Swithin's their christening day, if it rains?'
> 'Yes, dear. Ah me! I have not been to a christening
> for these many years; the baby's name was George, I
> remember – after the King.'
> 'I hear that King George is still staying at the town
> here. I *hope* he'll stay till I have seen him!'
> 'He'll wait till the corn turns yellow; he always does.'

'How *very* fashionable yellow is getting for gloves just now!'

'Yes. Some persons wear them to the elbow, I hear.'

'Do they? I was not aware of that. I struck my elbow last week so hard against the door of my aunt's mansion that I feel the ache now.' (Chap.17)

The idiolects are so marked that Hardy does not need to name the speakers. Of course they begin by talking about the weather. Matilda's dottiness is an only slightly exaggerated version of any hard-pressed conversationalist, not to mention a social aspirant, in an embarrassing situation, her hostess's polite resilience keeps them going, and the exaggerated free association is fun. The disjunctive habit is self-generative like any other and Matilda's polite contributions and nearly free associations get more bizarre as after a courteous show of local interest at the start she desperately seizes superficial cues and dashes headlong at yellow gloves and banged elbows. The running joke about her social self-promotions – 'my aunt's mansion' – is unobtrusive because the creaking structure of dialogue is an even better joke.

Hardy's conversation at its best is the exact opposite of this, well-matched and collaborative duets, with impromptu interaction. They are generative models, resembling artistic form or making a microcosm within the narrative. However individualized the participants – evenly or unevenly matched in narrative prowess, loquacious, subdued or silent – they resemble or represent aspects or elements of mind, bilaterally animated, mutually creative.

Sometimes the dialogue looks more like a competition than a cooperation, but opponents as well as allies egg each other on. There is an elegant example of this in the last chapter of *The Woodlanders* when a rustic chorus of narrators takes us from the reunited civilized couple,

Grace and Fitzpiers, to the woodland elegeist Marty South. The transitional conversation includes good telling and listening from the band of woodlanders, the anonymous barkripper, the hollow-turner, John Upjohn, Farmer Cawtree, Creedle, Giles's man, and a nameless boy who is nicely tucked into the final chorus with the reminder that he had assisted at Giles's Christmas party long ago. They eat, drink and rest from their redundant search-party labours, meditating on the ways of women as Melbury waits restlessly outside the door of the inn, looking gloomily to his daughter's future, 'it's a forlorn hope . . . and God knows how it will end!' In contrast and commentary, from deep experience and mature detachment, the three main speakers relax to tell brief marriage-stories, wittily, comically, and stylishly.

There is a thematic chain started by introductory remarks, the barkripper's, 'I'd gie her a good shaking if she was my maid; pretending to go out in garden, and leading folk a dozen-mile traipse that have got to get up at five o'clock . . .', the hollow-turner's criticism of the couple making 'a country talk about their parting for ever', and Creedle's brief 'Ah, young women do wax wanton in these days!'. The slight shift away from the particular instigates the main performances from the trio. The accomplished stories are smoothly linked: Creedle's wish that Grace had kept to Giles invokes Cawtree's example of the common 'deceiving of folks . . . in matrimony', his relations who quarrelled violently one minute and sang 'The Spotted Cow' the next, peaceful as 'two holy twins' and supporting each other in the high notes like 'street ballet-singers'. The barkripper's illustration of this theme of reconciliation is a husband returned after twenty-four years to laconic talk and domestic silence, found with his wife 'by the neighbours sound asleep in their chairs, not having known what to talk about at all'. This is topped by a three-handed exchange about the

cleverness of Mr and Mrs Fitzpiers, which inspires but
retards Upjohn's last story, prefaced with his objection to
the hollow-turner's view that women are getting cleverer:
'What they knowed then was not small . . . Always a
good deal more than the men'. His exemplary tale is
about his wife's profile, how she led him with wheelings
and turnings 'like a blind ram. . . . in the third climate of
our courtship', always keeping him on her pretty side.
The narrative ensemble is skilfully foreshortened, and
wound down by Upjohn's dry refusal to relate the full
chronicle of courtship, 'tis quite unnecessary'. Then they
return to the subject of the Fitzpiers reunion, and the
novelist modulates from cynical marriage tales to Marty's
faithful memories, as she laments the 'good man who did
good things'. The skilfully linked stories are amusing in
themselves – the story of the husband's return might be a
contracted version of something from *Wessex Tales* or *A
Group of Noble Dames*.

Such evenhanded conversations, in the fiction and
poetry, are open, exploratory and analytic, constructions of
inspirational meetings and oppositions, generative forms,
wholes greater than the sum of their cleverly connected
parts. Of course some of them are more analytic and
abstract than the woodlanders' choric narrative, like the
discussion of history between Angel and Tess. It also
illustrates the art of conversation. This conversation turns
on the marked contrast of idiolect, and shows Hardy's
lyrical prose. Like Marty's elegy, the language of Tess
shows Hardy the poet becoming Hardy the novelist in a
way which makes a comparison of his genres redundant: as
he wrote in the 'Sala delle Muse', prose and poetry speak
one heart and brain, 'extern to thee nothing'.

As I have said, Tess is given a lyrical and inventive
language, Angel a dull conventional prose, but Hardy
imagines them truly talking to each other, imagining each
other and re-imagining the world as speech connects and

responds. Each is intelligent and closely attentive to the other, but urgently pressing their own point-of-view, the educated man wanting to improve the less educated woman, and the woman harshly uttering her sense of history, class and gender. (I need not stress how Victorian both are, in form and content of their historical conscious-ness.) The argument Hardy invents for them is imagina-tive, because their speech is directed towards a perceived listener, and they imagine for the self and the other. Speech is imagined as partial, and shaped as functional, by the artist trying to give both sides. This may seem obvious, but it is surprising how many intellectual argu-ments in fiction, even in George Eliot or Tolstoy, for instance, are closed from the start, and clearly loaded.

These conversations between Tess and Angel spring naturally and immediately from action, and there is gen-eralization from particulars on both sides, common ground as well as obvious difference. Tess is a lyricist and imagist; moves in and out of dialect; her 'seems' demote metaphor to simile; she has an ear for simple, dignified, musical forms. Angel is slightly facetious, patronizing but sympathetically probing, an educated speaker, at ease with colloquialism, using blunter lexis, cruder phrases and some banal commonplaces. He is obliquely criticized but pre-sented with some sympathy, as a sincere participant in thought. The conversation is composed of promptings, questions and answers, suggestions and doubts. He is drawing her out, and she is talking to him and to herself, at times backing off to think. (They both do this, but Tess more often.)

Hardy is registering various moves in thoughtful and mutually constructive conversation. Its flow is colloquial, with subverbal exclamations like 'Oh','Ah!' and 'Eh?', brief often verbless sentences, and moves into the inter-locutor's territory. Tess's lyrical explanation, nicely calcu-lated as turning on a slight misunderstanding, emerges from a dynamic collaboration, a model for generative dialogue in and outside novels:

> 'What makes you draw off in that way, Tess? . . . Are you afraid?'
>
> 'Oh no, sir . . . not of outdoor things; especially just now when the apple-blooth is falling, and everything so green.'
>
> 'But you have your indoor fears – eh?'
>
> 'Well – yes, sir.'
>
> 'What of?'
>
> 'I couldn't quite say.'
>
> 'The milk turning sour?'
>
> 'No.'
>
> 'Life in general?'
>
> 'Yes, sir.'
>
> 'Ah – so have I, very often. This hobble of being alive is rather serious, don't you think so?'
>
> 'It is – now you put it that way.'
>
> 'All the same, I shouldn't have expected a young girl like you to see it so just yet. How is it you do?'
>
> She maintained a hesitating silence.
>
> 'Come, Tess, tell me in confidence.'
>
> She thought he meant what were the aspects of things to her, and replied shyly –
>
> 'The trees have inquisitive eyes, haven't they? – that is, seem as if they had. And the river says, – "Why do ye trouble me with your looks?" And you seem to see numbers of to-morrows just all in a line, the first of them the biggest and clearest, the others getting smaller and smaller as they stand farther away; but they all seem very fierce and cruel and as if they said, "I'm coming! Beware of me! Beware of me!"' (Chap. 19)

In *A Pair of Blue Eyes* Elfride's conversations with Henry Knight, the third man in her love life, also reveal gender and character but demonstrate a different kind of exchange. Elfride is intelligent, undereducated and scatty, trying and failing to hold her own in the face of a conventional man's bullying. Soon after they meet, Knight patronizes her novel-writing, saying she could do better by sticking to domestic scenes, and discourages her, 'That a young woman has taken to writing is not by any means the best thing to hear about her', and 'her greatest real praise, when the novelty of her inauguration has worn off, is that nothing happens to keep the talk of her alive' (Chap. 17). He stops attending and goes on with his train of thought while she seizes something he says and goes off on hers, in a model of conversational pauses, moves and distances. The talk is personal in feeling and motive, and at least once involves a discussion of ideas – about gender, ambition, writing fiction and non-fiction. Their later dialogues are less intellectual, more simply emotional in subject and conflict, but their construction brings out differences of gender, education and social expectation, through manner not matter.

Like the novel, the conversations are tragi-comic. Elfride is pathetic, silly, feckless and sympathetic, pro-voked by Knight's possessive demands to tell incompetent and forgiveable lies. She is incompetent because she is not thinking, letting spontaneity rule, not taught to sustain reason and master what Coleridge called the surview which marks educated speech. Knight's logical question-ing is harsh, hard and inexorable; he uses his education and logic oppressively, and he is less honest than she is because he is a self-deceiver. He presses and she evades, offending against the spirit but not the letter, and in the end he gets the answers he deserves.

Hardy skilfully shapes another long conversation where the identity of the speaker is never in doubt. The conflict of talk is conspicuous: this is war in which the enemies are unequally armed, and where the moral victory goes to the victim. It is also a study in the psychology of lying: it takes two to make a lie, and some lies are necessary. There are stage-directions, but repeated qualifications and the strong punctuation more subtly mark the speakers' hesitancy and slow pace:

> '. . . have you ever had a lover? I am almost sure you have not; but, have you?'
> 'Not, as it were, a lover; I mean, not worth mention-ing, Harry,' she faltered.
> 'Still he was a lover?'
> 'Well, a sort of lover, I suppose,' she responded tardily.
> 'A man, I mean, you know.'
> 'Yes; but only a mere person, and – '
> 'But truly your lover?'
> 'Yes; a lover certainly – he was that. Yes, he might have been called my lover.'
> . . . .
> 'You don't mind, Harry, do you?'. . . .
> 'Of course, I don't seriously mind. In reason, a man cannot object to such a trifle. I only thought you hadn't – that was all.' (Chap. 30)

This is the first of three conversations in which serial interrogation drives Elfride to confess. Here she is holding off by evasion and omission, but she soon begins to give way, when she finds her telltale long-lost earring and in a second dialogue Knight 'wrings' out the secret of her previous engagement. The third interrogation drives her not just to equivocate but lie – 'probably' as the scrupu-lous or evasive narrator says, not intending 'a wilful prevarication' but 'in a confusion of ideas'. The timing and spacing, like that in the interrogations of Koestler' s *Darkness at Noon*, shows Hardy's insight into brainwashing.

Knight is intent on possessing a woman without any past at all, and he says insincerely that he wants to know about her old admirer because it would embitter their lives if he turned up. She reassures him spontaneously, digging a hole for herself, that it 'cannot be', he asks 'sharply' 'Why not?', and she answers carelessly and spontaneously:

> 'If he's dead, how can you meet him?'
> 'Is he dead? Oh, that's different altogether!'. . . . 'But let me see – what did you say about that tomb and him?'
> 'That's his tomb,' she continued faintly.
> 'What! was he who lies buried there your lover?' . . .
> 'Yes; and I didn't love him or encourage him.'
> 'But you let him kiss you – you said so, you know, Elfride.'
> She made no reply.
> 'Why. . . . you surely said you were in some degree engaged to him. . . . And I have been fancying you said – I am almost sure you did – that you were sitting with him *on* that tomb. Good God! . . . are you telling me untruths?'

Several sentences later he is very angry and she is very shaken:

> 'Did you say you were sitting on that tomb?' . . .
> 'Yes; and it was true.'
> 'Then how, in the name of Heaven, can a man sit upon his own tomb?'
> 'That was another man. Forgive me, Harry, won't you?'
> 'What, a lover in the tomb, and a lover on it?'
> 'O – O – yes!'

'Then there were two before me?'
'I – suppose so.' (Chap. 32)

She makes a fool of herself but so does he; their foolish dialogues are amusing; but more. Writing comic dialogue, creating sympathy, plotting, creating the tensions of argument and articulating character, Hardy is once more generating dialogues in which one mind presses another. He plots the moves, backwards, forwards and sideways, straight and oblique, fast or slow, one square or more at a time. Chess is a supporting model,. with its rules and rituals, characters and wars, passions and aesthetic purity. Her father says Elfride plays chess quite well 'for a woman', and her games with her lovers have several functions, but in conversation she is defeated because she cannot make the knight's move, only the pawn's. The dialogues are comic and political. Elfride cannot hold past and present together, as she is pressed and oppressed in conversation until she can only think of one thing at a time and then cannot think at all.

She is broken down and the sexual tyranny which makes her lie punishes her for telling the truth. Like Jane Austen, Hardy can stage a comic social scene to represent a more serious exchange or conflict. In these dialogues he is interested in the power structure of interrogation and confession, truthtelling and lying. The political implications of these dialogues bring out the novel's larger critique of sexism, which Hardy may not have been entirely conscious of making. Knowledge of a biographical connection between Elfride and Emma reinforces the sense of feminist sympathies but the novel speaks for itself, especially when its characters speak to each other. (I do not suggest that Hardy is never sexist, and there are comments which his narrator makes about his heroine which might come from Knight. Hardy occasionally patronizes her and is soft about her softness in a way he never is with Tess – who is not soft, though she and Elfride both die tragically because they are women.) The dramatic dialogues, here and in Tess, and in other novels too, show Hardy imaginatively constructing a sexual dialectic, and a larger dialectic also: the concept of conversation highlights a sense of otherness and a sense of communication.

The importance and prevalence of conversation in the poetry shows a cross-over from the novels. Here too the conversational form is structurally functional and implicitly analytic. 'Her Second Husband Hears her Story' tells the grotesque tale – and tells the tale of its laconic telling – about a woman who sews up her drunken husband in a sheet, to avoid his embrace. The first narrator is her second husband, who begins in *medias res* with a stunned summary of what she has just told him, in bed:

> Still, Dear, it is incredible to me
>   That here, alone,
> You should have sewed him up until he died . . .

The history of motive and action, with some particulars, is elicited, regularly interrupted with incredulous, and far from disinterested, commentary by the victim's successor: 'And in this very bed', 'It's a strange tale!', 'And this same bed?' and 'Did you intend his death by your tight lacing?'. He meets refusal, 'that I cannot own' and a repetition of motive, not reassuring 'I could not think of else that would avail'. His final understated 'Well, it's a cool queer tale!' leaves strong reverberations, especially given the narrative location, 'this very bed', and his mild ingratiating marital 'Dear', contrasted with the wife's complete lack of personal address as she tells. The poem leaves untold the occasion for the fascinating anaphrodisiac pillowtalk. The form of conversation makes this story: it is told in a particular place to a particular listener, and what is impressive is not just the death, but also this telling. The second husband's presence make the wife's tale a little less sympathetic and a little grimmer. From title to conclusion, it is a gem of black comedy, which combines suggestive intensity with as much self-reference – given its scale – as the title and ending of *The Winter's Tale*.

Another listener and significant response are characterized in another grim comedy, 'The Ruined Maid', where narrative is also clearly directed to a chosen particular ear, the innocent and deprived country girl's. As in 'Her Second Husband Hears' the teller is dominant but the response of a spellbound listener equally important. In part it is stated, but also slyly, and more strikingly, implied. What has been called the silent partner in a conversation – here as in many cases, the more silent partner – not only determines the dominant act of storytelling but suggests its consequence, taking the narrative forward and opening the ending. Hardy loves conversations about events which have changed the life of the teller but whose telling changes the life of the listener too. The listener implies envious admiration from the beginning, but becomes more impressed, 'now I'm bewitched', and 'I wish I had feathers, a fine sweeping gown . . .'. She is poor, silly, and like little Em'ly would like to be a lady. So what will stop her? 'The Ruined Maid' is a party-piece always read for laughs, but it is possible to read it less innocently – listening to reverberations – as the doubly ironic story of a sinister conversation where a susceptible girl arrives in London and is seduced – or at the very least, obviously seducible – by a prostitute.

One of Hardy's most subversive conversational poems is 'The Monument-Maker', already discussed, in which the artist allows his memorial to be criticized, and is surprised into a kind of dialogue. The form of conversation is displaced and undermined. The poem begins as a monologue but is answered by a second voice, the poem buries that second voice, then resurrects it, and the two speakers join language and share a subject but do not always address each other directly. Hardy sets together voices that address and miss each other in a way entirely appropriate to the subject of an inadequate, rejected monument and an inadequate, rejected love. The mourning survivor narrates not to the dead woman but, first hopefully and then plaintively, about her, and she speaks dismissively and scornfully, about him, interrupting and contradicting his story. Her intervention makes the story of the monument the story of the poem itself: he appropriates her story in his monument, she denies and upsets the appropriation, and ends up appropriating the poem. Its memorial praise is thwarted and his last speech tails off weakly, addressed well-meaningly to the reader.

'The Haunter' is a conversation poem which shows why Hardy wrote 'The Monument-Maker'. There is a similar pattern of a male speaker's narrative and a woman character's inset speech, but here the woman is made to confirm the man's expectations and give the desired answer, in a blatant wish-fulfilment. The dialogue has obviously been set up, and is really a thinly disguised monologue, like so much fictitious dialogue. Indeed, in a sense all literature is disguised monologue, but there is usually the more-or-less well-imagined presence of otherness. There is also, in successfully dramatic literary work, an apparent openness to the unpremeditated or unprecedented event or feeling, an access to the unconscious – not Freud's unconscious, but the more exciting, ethically free, enabling unconscious mind conceived of before Freud, in the work of such psychologists as Coleridge, the reflex of mind or unconscious cerebration.

What Hardy's invention also examines most profoundly

and passionately, is the conversational exchange between a detached spectator and a speaker intensely articulating an experience. Arnold hit on the great phrase, 'the dialogue of the mind with itself', and Hardy wrote the poetry of that dialogue. The divided mind is necessary to the telling of certain stories. In some of these conversations between someone who is involved and someone who is more detached, he ironically contrasts knowledge and ignorance, pointing a case by stylized or exaggerated antithesis. Sometimes the detached voice is characterized as superior, impersonal or supernatural. It may be aptly anonymous, a god or a fate or Time or a force of nature or an anonymous wisdom, like the repeated voice of history 'At Lulworth Cove a Hundred Years Ago'. The mysterious masked figure in the Beckett-like 'The Masked Face' is an ironic Authority who puts down the human innocent. It is anonymous and speaks with a weighty detachment which is not cold but very remote. Both speakers seem to be somewhere beyond human limits, before or after life, but are not:

> I found me in a great surging space,
>   At either end a door,
> And I said: 'What is this giddying place,
>   With no firm-fixéd floor,
>   That I knew not of before?'
> 'It is Life,' said a mask-clad face.

The disembodied masked face, like the location, is made physically strange, by the mask, the mask's 'said', and later by 'a bleak' smile. It answers the human questions unflatteringly but not ruthlessly, and instructively, 'There was once complained a goosequill pen. . . . / Of the words it had to write / Because they were past its ken'. Hardy is using the right image for the person as for the place because he is trying to write past his ken, to imagine the more than human. He is the writer imagining himself instrumental as the familiar pen, slightly lowered by 'goose' but given speech, and while admitting ignorance ('past its ken') saying truly that we write more than we understand. Probably here, in a life-lamenting fable which grows less simple than it first seems, no doubt for writer as well as reader.

Another of these authoritative abstractions is the speaker in 'Who's in the Next Room?', again in conversation with a merely human being. It is a conversation too austere to be called compassionate, though it makes us feel that odd pity or sorrow, both egoistic and empathetic, for the common lot. The poem is an exchange between knowledge and ignorance, in an impassioned episode when Death has come close to the main speaker, who engrosses four lines in each five-line verse, leaving the last line for the reply. In the first three verses the questioner, who 'seemed to see', hear, and feel the presence in the next room, is told that he did not. By the end it is evident that the wrong questions are asked. The final exchange is gravely different. All the questions are answered in the affirmative, as the speaker stops thinking in terms of his senses, and about the past and present:

> 'A figure wan
> With a message to one in there of something due?
> Shall I know him anon?'

He seizes the implications of what's in the next room to imagine the future, beginning to answer his own questions, as we do in finding the right ones, the guesses laconically endorsed in the chilling last line. By then he knows 'the next room' is a metaphor, and who is there, and so do we: 'Yea he; and he brought such; and you'll know him anon'.

This is the voice of Hardy's irony, solemnly and

patiently spelling it all out, not pitying but invoking the sense of mortality in a voice which comes frighteningly from nowhere, unidentified except as a source of knowledge. Like other voices in Hardy, it seems not human but speaks as something deep in the questioner, an intuitive knowledge. This is another dynamic conversation, between ignorance and knowledge, in which the teller changes the listener, and a sympathetic displacement of elegy.

In 'You on the Tower' we have a more predictable dialogue. A factory owner too busy to be on the watch questions someone on his factory tower. The anonymous voice first forms the answers by repeating the question, changing only pronouns, and giving an impression of relaxation and calm. He assures the busy man with no time to watch but anxious for Enjoyment, that Enjoyment is on the wing. The message comes 'He still is flying on'. Finally questioned by the man, desperate and sweating, in labour or illness or death, the surprised watchman regrets that he is too late, disclosing his own detached preoccupation with the skies:

> 'Hoi, Watchman! I'm here. When comes he?
>   Between my sweats I am chill.'
>   – 'Oh you there, working still?
> Why, surely he reached you a time back,
>   And took you miles from your mill?
> He duly came in his winging,
>   And now he has passed out of view.
> How can it be that you missed him?
>   He brushed you by as he flew.'

The moral conclusion and feeling are deepened and complicated by the shift of role. The owner seems to assume that the man on the tower is his factory watchman, but it is eventually clear that he is not: 'Oh you there . . .?' He is a watcher of the skies rather than the owner's affairs, he has assumed he left the factory, and though he carelessly says he saw Enjoyment brush by, he did not notice the missed moment. This neat sinister turn completes the conversation and compounds the parable, to make it more wide-ranging, more moral and more political, as the Watchman's insouciance coolly throws into relief human egocentricity, as well as inattentive human hope. These abstractions have emotions and habits, and there is something amusing and neat about an exchange between two such careless beings.

Another voice which is impersonal and knowing but endowed with personality is Hardy's composite Muse, in 'Rome: The Vatican: Sala delle Muse' (mentioned in my first chapter). She is gleaming marble, but Hardy endows her with charm and beauty, though 'her small sweet marvellous face' is all Muse. Her voice is affectionate, sympathetic, grave but slightly amused: 'Be not perturbed'; she and her sisters are all the same, man-made. This is doubly true since she is a character in his poem:

> . . . 'I am projected from thee,
> One that out of thy brain and heart thou causest to be –
> Extern to thee nothing.'

She is abstract and individual, rational and loving, as a Muse must be, beginning an emotionally flexible conversation as she comes down from her plinth, 'Regarded so long, we render you sad?', to soothe the genre-racked artist, swayed – but she says 'swayed' is the wrong word – by Form, Tune, Story, Dance and Hymn. She is the only one of Hardy's abstract wisdoms to have charm, as a Muse should.

These are impersonal, superhuman, questioners, but the necessary provoker or instigator who comes from outside is often personal, dramatized as a interlocutor with some identity, who preserves the poem from soliloquy, making it a true dramatic monologue, a voice which speeds and shapes narrative into the energy of answer by the curiosity of question or the voice of wonder, questioning a mystery or puzzle. As we see, Hardy likes conversation-poems where the listener is changed, subtly and perhaps ambiguously, but where we concentrate on the telling and do not immediately read the stealthy implications of the listening. In many poems Hardy sets strangers talking. In 'The Memorial Brass 186 – ' the chief character, a weeping widow, is cross-questioned by a young student of church architecture. He is sketched with a light hand, and his interest elicits her tragic–comic story of romantic illusion and marriage:

> 'Why do you weep there, O sweet lady,
> Why do you weep before that brass? –
> (I'm a mere student sketching the mediaeval)'

She relates her vow to be faithful, rashly imprinted in her married name on ironically memorial brass, her change of heart and her fear of the new betrothed. The story evokes its last line, his naïvely sanguine, 'Madam, I swear your beauty will disarm him!', which like his 'O sweet' (less superficially balladlike than it may seem) and his flattering assumption that she is not a widow ('Your father's?') fixes this unreliable listener. His innocence is a foil and offers a useless response to the silly impulsive lady. Threatened by a husband's power and afraid to tell her past, she is a Hardy heroine in brief, whose history might have expanded into a short story, like 'On the Western Circuit', also about rash imagination, or a novel. The conversation shows Hardy's thorough motivation, the impulsive lady confiding in the susceptible stranger revealingly drawn to the mediaeval. She is text and he is subtext, in a feat of compression equalled only by the tale of a night call by 'The Sailor's Mother'. The story explains her behaviour. Her son, effectively and plausibly never said to be dead, can only know their old house and its new occupant seems not to hear him. The questioning promotes and retards the story, which is particularized by emotions, not characters. Like much naïve story-telling, her narrative is over-allusive, and its unexplained 'heard' and 'him', marks of uneducated speech, provoke questions to elicit, not the whole, but the core story. It is told in a solemn colloquial poetry, the speech-rhythms drawn out with Hardy's prosaic-sounding lyricism, especially in the long lines, here, but not in other stanzas, slow fourteeners:

> 'O whence do you come,
> Figure in the night-fog that chills me numb?'
> 'I come to you across from my house up there,
> And I don't mind the brine-mist clinging to me
>   That blows from the quay,
> For I heard him in my chamber, and thought you
>   unaware.'

>   'But what did you hear,
> That brought you so blindly knocking in this middle-
> watch so drear?'

Hardy's topos of provisionality is adapted to pathos, 'My sailor son's voice as 'twere calling at your door'. The rational 'Nobody's nigh!' – 'nobody' is repeated three times in the ghost-hungry poem – is drearily accepted at the end, present and past closed in a disappointment familiar from *Jude*: 'And the salt fog mops me. And nobody's come'. As well as eliciting a story of painfully tender love – as love tends to be in Hardy – the interlocutor's address makes the woman as strange as her tale: she has bare feet, skeletal figure and sunk eyes. Her own style is physical but haunted by oddity and ambiguity: domestic vivid 'mops', brine-mist suggestively 'clinging', and 'chills me numb' – fog or figure?

A similar strangeness marks the question and answer of a more ordinary event in 'Penance', where an undefined speaker wonders why a 'pale thin man' sits at an old cold harpsichord in a fireless room and is told that when the keys were active and the fire lit a woman used to play there, alone, and he is doing now what he neglected once. One of Hardy's most remorseful lyrics, it has a clever grisly transmutation at the end as the keys become dead teeth. In another haunting both strange and physical, repulsive and desired, vehicle and tenor unexpectedly clash together in the brown, dead, loose ivories, death is ordered and repressed into simile, or felt stirring, even in simile:

> . . . and the chill old keys,
> Like a skull's brown teeth
> Loose in their sheath,
> Freeze my touch; yes freeze.

'In the British Museum' similarly contrasts the outside and inside view, this time of an educated and a less educated speaker, presenting another action which strikes an observer as strange, evoking question and story. On this occasion it is not a personal emotion which is striking but the wondering response of historical imagination, conveyed and compounded by the wondering response in the question:

> 'What do you see in that time-touched stone,
>   When nothing is there
> But ashen blankness, although you give it
>   A rigid stare?'

The sympathetic curious sharer, closely observing the close observer, refines the response:

> 'You look not quite as if you saw,
>   But as if you heard,
> Parting your lips, and treading softly
>   As mouse or bird.'

After receiving redundant information about the Areopagus, the labouring man, as he calls himself, explains with apologies for lack of art and learning, that he 'can't help thinking' the stone has echoed the voice of Paul.

> 'Paul as he stood and preached beside it
>   Facing the crowd
> A small gaunt figure with wasted features . . .'

The poem uses the teller's auto-didacticism to emphasize imagination, but delicately, as it is filtered through the impression made on the questioner, and on the reader in his imaginative particulars. It is an impressive story of the historical consciousness, and the social point links it with Hardy's feelings about educational deprivation, as a genuine passion for history contrasts with the cultivated man's museum-knowledge, 'It is only the base of a pillar, they'll tell you'. Hardy does not labour the irony, and the touch of class is the more moving for being part of a larger concern and not overstated. Telling and listening have an air of immediacy, and the two parts are simply set side by side, as dialogue, neither speaker being given narrative authority. The two meet as strangers but share an experience. The poem is a dialogue of two imaginations.

In 'The Workbox', the characters are husband and wife, but speak as strangers to each other. The dialogue-poem concentrates on secrecy and emotional distance, but shows the disadvantage of not leaving conversation alone to make its impact. After an exchange between an innocent husband and his wife with a past, Hardy adds a narrator's comment which is obtrusive even though – perhaps because – it tries to sound reserved. A powerful poem loses power because Hardy adds to the implicit dialogue, and would have done much better without its last verse, which was probably appended to quieten the strident irony of the wife's protestation:

> 'Ah, no. I should have understood!
>   It shocked you that I gave
> To you one end of a piece of wood
>   Whose other is in a grave?'
>
> 'Don't, dear, despise my intellect,
>   Mere accidental things
> Of that sort never have effect
>   On my imaginings.'
>
> Yet still her lips were limp and wan,
>   Her face still held aside,
> As if she had known not only John,
>   But known of what he died.

'Under the Waterfall' begins spontaneously with a narrator whose memory has just been jogged, speaking to an undesignated interlocutor:

> 'Whenever I plunge my arm, like this,
> In a basin of water, I never miss
> The sweet sharp sense of a fugitive day,
> Fetched back from its thickening shroud of grey.
>   Hence the only prime
>   And real love-rhyme . . .'

What is brought back is the sound of a little 'valley fall', but more explanation is required by the listener, who repeats the narrator's words to ask a question, and changes them as we do in composing the fluency of talk.

'And why gives this the only prime
Idea to you of a real love-rhyme?
And why does plunging your arm in a bowl
Full of spring water, bring throbs to your soul?'

The metrical shift and slight conceptual variation – 'idea . . . of' instead of simply 'prime and real love-rhyme' – bring in and introduce the questioner's new development: the abstraction of 'prime and real love-rhyme', spring water for water, and the addition of throbs and soul. The interlocutor encourages and energizes the answer, begun by the responsive filler, 'Well', tells the story of the lost drinking-glass. The dialogue illustrates and dramatizes two distinct and cooperative aspects of mind. The habits of conversation are observed, a story is dynamically and flexibly told, and imaginative action is modelled – this is how people talk and how poetry gets written.

The sense of abstraction can be especially strong in conversation-poems like this, whose lyrical drama permits a vagueness or abstraction of persons and place impossible in a guided narration. This poem is curiously suspended, sexless and spaceless. We do not know that the first speaker is a woman until the penultimate line, 'No lip has touched it since his and mine' and we do not know to whom she is speaking, only that she is washing her hands in company. That leaf-patterned earthenware is very Victorian, but strangely isolated from any domestic context, and transformed into a sacred place and object. The conversational language and tone are stylized by the refrains and strong rhythm, finally rising into a chant or

incantation appropriate to the sense of ritual. The structure of conversation is naturalistic, but isolates the story,
helping to make it awed and sacramental.

'On the Departure Platform' is a conversation of
strangers where the listener makes an unexpected appearance. The speaker laments the moment of parting from
his love, a moment lost because it is emotionally unique,
unrepeatable. He seems to be talking to himself, in the
personal reverie of lyric, till a stranger interrupts his
privacy, suddenly, and for one question only. The sense
of an interrupted structure is underlined by the speech
marks, which are used only for the second voice, as if the
first voice was solely responsible for the poem until the
surprise entry in the sixth stanza:

> And in season she will appear again –
> Perhaps in the same soft white array –
> But never as then!
>
> – 'And why, young man, must eternally fly
> A joy you'll repeat, if you love her well?'

Again the questioning, two lines by an interested listener, conspicuously extends the poem: it sums up feeling,
names feeling, generalizes, and adds the intensifiers of
'eternally' and 'joy'. The question introduces a retarding
commonsensical objection, 'but why?' provokes re-affir-
mation. There is no elaborate incident here, only a
momentary intense and imaginative feeling, strengthened
into generalization and sad disclaimer. Through conversation, the slight incident is made to develop, and the
speaker goes beyond what he first said, stimulated into
articulating or implying the ineffable:

> O friend, nought happens twice thus; why,
> I cannot tell!

The second voices in the last two poems are demurring
and questioning, 'But why gives this . . .?' and 'And why,
young man?' They are the voices of strangers who
become familiars in the course of conversation, sympathetic but commonsensical, interrogating intensities they
find strange or puzzling. The questioner 'In the Moonlight' is less sensitive, and the conversation nicely contrasts
his conventional expectations with a strange deep truth
which bursts out in response. 'O lonely workman, standing there/ In a dream' begins the friendly observer,
impressed by the importunate gaze and making a joke
about it raising a 'phantom', to be told that the gazer
would rather see that ghost than 'all the living.' Provoking
another assumption that she was his great love he gives
the bitter explanation, 'Nay: she was the woman I did not
love'. The emotional outburst is motivated and urged by
the conventional enquirer, who is put down by the
unexpected like the sympathetic speaker in 'We Are
Seven'.

Every attempt to group these many conversations
brings out the individuality of each form. Artistic self-
consciousness and passionate intensity strengthen each
other in the complex emotion and story-telling of 'The
Whitewashed Wall' where both teller and listener stand
outside the main action. The narrative begins as
questioning:

> Why does she turn in that shy soft way
>   Whenever she stirs the fire,
> And kiss to the chimney-corner wall
>   As if entranced to admire
> Its whitewashed bareness more than the sight
>   Of a rose in richest green?
> I have known her long, but this raptured rite
>   I never before have seen.

– Well, once when her son cast his shadow there,
    A friend took a pencil and drew him
Upon that flame-lit wall. And the lines
    Had a lifelike semblance to him.
And there long stayed his familiar look;
    But one day, ere she knew,
The whitener came to cleanse the nook,
    And covered the face from view.

'Yes,' he said: 'My brush goes on with a rush,
    And the draught is buried under;
When you have to whiten old cots and brighten,
    What else can you do, I wonder?'
But she knows he's there. And when she yearns
    For him, deep in the labouring night,
She sees him as close at hand, and turns
    To him under his sheet of white.

The outside report preserves the painful tender emotion, in narrative kept wholly behaviouristic. The mother says nothing, neither does her son, but everything is there in gesture and movement. He cast a shadow, the artist drew it, the whitener obliterates it, and the mother, turns, looks and kisses, in speechless rites of love and constancy, 'she knows he's there', silence the more moving for being conveyed in the sensitively mediated words of an old acquaintance, 'I have known her long', but a stranger to her story. His distance brings reassurance, solidity, increased wonder, making him a reliable narrator of the raptured rite.

These speakers are not excluded by commonsense or ignorance, but they are spectators, standing outside the brilliantly minimal drama of four people – who represent love, art, work and death – at slightly different removes. The story's abstract quality is kept particular, as one speaks the familiar prompt, 'Why?' to be answered by the common starter, 'Well'. The story is told from the outside so intense emotions need not be named, as they are inferred from action, and the depth, delicacy, reserve and privacy of the action are respected, scrutinized but left intact. The speechless rites of drawing, erasure and remembrance are intensely appreciated, but earthed by the ordinary exchange of conversation. The tellers perform their acts of affectionate narrative, imaginatively. It is Hardy's benign gossip at its best.

In this poem, the wondering response aptly records the story of an emotion, and, by wondering, leaves a sensitive gap between the narrative attempt and the inner feeling, which is approached but not possessed and not named, except as yearning. The conversation is another model for the artist's communication, as well as one of Hardy's best articulations of love and loss. The outside view also avoids telling too much. We are told of loss, not death, and the suggestiveness of the whitener and the sheet of white are left to do their work.

As we have seen, Hardy's second voices nearly always come from outside the experience, almost from nowhere, almost from outside the poem, to ask good questions and renew memory or contemplation. (The few conversational elegies are marked exceptions.) Although he likes to bring listeners from outside, to the lyrical innerness, they are not remote or cold, but partake of the poetry, enter language and form, add an image or rephrase an idea, join in the generation of lyrical narrative. The second voice is subordinate but active. Of course Hardy did not invent such conversations, which are often found in ballads of all periods:

> 'As you came from the holy land
> Of Walsinghame,

Met you not with my true love
By the way as you came?'

This sixteenth-century poem, like the best imitations
of its form, Keats's mediaeval pastiche 'La Belle Dame
Sans Merci', Wordsworth's and Coleridge's lyrical ballads'We are Seven' and 'The Ancient Mariner', composes
a lyric interview which elegantly demonstrates the uncertainty principle, that to observe is to change the matter
observed. As question urges answer, it gets the answer it
deserves. Hardy's interviews in poetry usually dramatize a
more subdued questioner than Wordsworth and Coleridge, more like the muted interested presences in 'As
you came from the holy land' or 'La Belle Dame', who
motivate the storytelling, give more substance and detail
to the teller's character and situation, and shape beginning,
tension and end, in a defined act of telling something for
a specific listener, questioner and occasion. Like the
amazed wondering audiences at the end of Shakespeare's
romances, who beg Prospero, Imogen and Paulina to
clear up the mystery and satisfy speculation, their wonder
is functional as well as apt. The wonder of the reader is
represented and compounded by the wonder of the
character in the poem.

One or two of Hardy's delicate lyrical narratives are
not conversations in the ordinary sense of the word, but
conversational absences or evasions, like the skilfully light-
toned 'At the Railway Station, Upway' in which one
person speaks and the other sings. Words turn to music as
a boy's kind offer of cheer, 'I can play my fiddle to you'
is made good and he plays. The convict says nothing, but
his response is vigorous:

And the man in the handcuffs suddenly sang
With grimful glee:

'This life so free
Is the thing for me!'

This poem is about imaginative conversation, in several ways. It heartwarmingly seizes a moment of goodwill, a human grace which is communicated to bestow a brief freedom. The boy impulsively and warmly speaks and performs, even the handcuffed man and the constable smile, and gratitude for a gift of music moves the prisoner to creative and responsive song. There is irony, but it is kept down by the genuine good feeling, and seasons the happening which could have been and is so far from being mawkish. This conversation of strangers is an odd life-affirming meeting and exchange, in which the traditional union of words and music is made deep and strange. (It may remind us of the first chapters of *Great Expectations* and the current of kindness that flows from Pip to Magwitch as the convict gobbles his meal.) The poem imagines and isolates a single moment with a peculiar sadness and strength, discovering what conversation can be and do, and also, though it seems clumsy and unnecessary to generalize such loving particulars, what love and art can do. Like 'The Whitewashed Wall' it is intensely particular but strikingly metonymic, leaving us with the feeling that all human life is there.

A love poem which says much for the sweetness and harshness of Hardy's imagination, it imagines a communion of strangers which is more expressive of intimate reciprocal exchange, wellwishing, offered and accepted kindness, than any of his poems about love between man and woman. It belongs with another tender poem, also not exactly a conversation, which speaks as if there were no such thing as a stranger. The unnamed emotion in 'To an Unborn Pauper Child' seems a little like Sue's love for Jude, which is scrupulously described by her husband Phillotson as 'a curious tender solicitude'. Hardy imagines a language for the complex feelings of imaginative love, for accepting any child as our own, urgently solicitous while knowing protection is impossible. The affectionate apostrophe is unheard and unanswerable.

In this stanza the only word not a monosyllable is 'common', used to describe the 'lot' which humanity at its most anonymous and poverty-stricken shares with the visionary 'songsinger'. Helpless before and helpless after birth, the creature is the more tenderly imagined, the more 'dear', because it is unborn, unnamed and ungendered:[1]

> Fain would I, dear, find some shut plot
> Of earth's wide wold for thee, where not
> > One tear, one qualm,
> > Should break the calm.
> But I am weak as thou and bare;
> No man can change the common lot to rare.

CHAPTER SIX

The Poetry of Place

Keats writes 'The poetry of earth is never dead' in 'The Grasshopper and the Cricket' and Coleridge discusses 'the poetry of nature' in *The Biographia Literaria*. It is possible that the familiar phrase 'poetry of place' first appears in 'After a Romantic Day', and it must be at least an early metaphorical suggestion. The poem is a brief love-lyric, so it is surprising that it finds room for such a self-conscious, complex, and ambiguous literary term. The whole poem is a surprise, highly emotional but analytic, its simple short teeming lines a telling refusal to tell all:

> The railway bore him through
> An earthen cutting out from a city:
>   There was no scope for view,
> Though the frail light shed by a slim young moon
>   Fell like a friendly tune.
>
> And the blank lack of any charm
>   Of landscape did no harm.
> The bald steep cutting, rigid, rough,
>   And moon-lit, was enough
> For poetry of place: its weathered face
> Formed a convenient sheet whereon
> The visions of his mind were drawn

The poem is clearly about place. The scene is sharply specified, though minimal in every aspect and layer: a bald railway cutting, fraily lit by the new moon, offering a blank space on which unspecified visions are traced.

The romance of the day is minimally announced in the title, the preposition 'After' announcing the evasion. We end with that explicit statement about an experience deemed to be sufficient for poetry of place.

The poem is a paradigm for place, in Hardy's work and outside it. It contemplates poetry of place in its two senses, one literal, the other metaphorical. 'Poetry of place' can mean a place which is the occasion for poetry, which inspires poetry or is used by it as subject or symbol. It also indicates a place, natural or man-made, which can be compared with poetry, and called poetic. Hardy seems to use it here in both senses.

Hardy himself did not ask the question, or make my distinction, rather asserting that meaning does not reside in place: 'The poetry of a scene' he wrote on August 23, 1865, for his memoir, *The Life of Thomas Hardy*, 'varies with the minds of the perceivers. Indeed, it does not lie in the scene at all'. This opinion ignores the inclinations of poets and painters, to admire and use recognizable beauties of landscape. Hardy is drawn to the shapes, colours and detail of the hills, heaths, foliage, rivers and seascape of Dorset and Cornwall, and when he makes poetry out of it in some of the elegies it is to seize on pleasurable elements.

His symbolic or significant scene is usually a natural beauty, sometimes with a man-made touch, as it is in 'After a Romantic Day'. Here there is poetry of place in the two senses. The poem is made as emotions are recollected in tranquillity, reformed and written, with the help of the scene outside through which he is moving, and then made conscious of itself. The occasion might be wholly or partly imagined, or it might also be exactly as the poem proposes, but either way the place is visually dominant, entirely displacing the remembered scenes of the day and the city. The railway cutting is not quite blank: bald, steep, with a young moon's light on its weathered face, and outside a city, it is observed by the narrator, a traveller returning from a romantic day in that city. It is endowed with an independent and individual life of its own, minimal but enough to inspire poetry in companionship and reciprocity, a meeting of subject and object. The poet says that the place itself has no visual appeal, but that is not true of the moonlight which lights it, whose famous charm is appreciated, beautified, and animated, in the images of slimness, youth and music.

The poem doubles the emotional reticence. The scene is conveniently unobtrusive and resonant in a special way. It limits resonance. If it were more spectacular or beautiful in colour and shape, like the sharply visualized Cornish cliffs and waves and skies needed in the elegies, it would be too expressive and tell too much of the romantic secret, more about the events and relationships of his day than he wants or needs to tell. An extra charm is given by the explicit and literary summing up in the understated figure, 'a convenient sheet'. The very lack of high compliment, the matter-of-fact thankyou to the place, is casual in tone but intense in effect, a final touch of reticence. Hardy's poetry of place fully explicates its own terminology, in a slyly humorous and imaginative way, gently putting place in its place.

'Wessex Heights' takes us from delighted reverie to harsh recall. It is one of Hardy's most bitter poems, compounding grief and grievance. Florence Hardy said it was written in deep distress at the reception of *Jude the Obscure* and always wrung her heart. In spite of its place-name title the Wessex heights are not particularized, though insistently and repeatedly named. They are said at the start to be adapted, or rather, typically, seem adapted, to the speaker's condition, 'For thinking, dreaming, dying on . . .'. The shapes of the hills are left unspecified and the few physical details describe the haunted places, to be shunned, 'the great grey Plain' and the 'tall-spired town',

but not the heights. Almost all we know about them is
their general locality and their upland feature. In a way
the very lack of specification implies familiarity, and this
is reinforced by the place names which give the effect of
a neighbourly nudging allusion, like saying 'you remember Ingpen' or 'I needn't describe Bulbarrow' – and
Bulbarrow is 'homely'.

These Wessex heights are not a totally blank or associa-
tionless place, and they are used by the reminiscent poet
to express what he might have been. His young self is not
a nothing, nor a conditioned and circumscribed creature,
but a potentiality, which his older self imagines naïvely
surprised by the later development. Hardy's young self
uses a mature epithet for casualty, 'crass', but the rest
of his free indirect sentence is strange and simple, like
him:

> Down there I seem to be false to myself, my simple
>   self that was,
> And is not now, and I see him watching, wondering
>   what crass cause
> Can have merged him into such a strange continuator
>   as this,
> Who yet has something in common with himself, my
>   chrysalis.

It is important that there are two places, polarized as
flatland and heights. The sharp division concentrates the
animosity in the lowland, where 'mind-chains clank', all
sour, hostile and frightening associations, and the freedom
on the heights, where his 'next neighbour is the sky', and
there are no associations – the complete lack of descriptive
detail endorses this. The feelings of acute anxiety and
dread are Kafkalike in strength and kind: passage barred
by hostile shadows and 'phantoms with weird detective
ways',[1] with a blurring of personal detail in the generalized

and enlarged hostile characters. The uninhabited heights
evoke relief and recognition made almost independent of
the imagining self. Almost but not quite independent,
because the place names are just touched by fondness,
two given the epithets, 'homely' and 'little', two with
their names repeated in the first and last stanzas. These
muted endearments and the repetition reinforce a final
release from the deep anxiety which marks the poem –
touched by paranoia. The final 'So' celebrates the high
places seeming 'shaped as if by a kindly hand', in Hardy' s
quiet agnostic version of the psalmist's 'I will lift up mine
eyes unto the hills':

> So I am found on Ingpen Beacon, or on Wyll's-Neck
>   to the west,
> Or else on homely Bulbarrow, or little Pilsdon
>   Crest . . .

Another restrained poem of place is 'Overlooking the
River Stour' (discussed in Chapter Four) where the rich
particularity of a natural scene, repeated and sharply
presented, slowly builds an anti-associative process, forming and reforming a scene which should not have
engrossed the attention. Donald Davie proposed[2] that the
artificial metaphors ('little crossbows animate', 'the curves
of an eight', and 'shavings of crystal spray','ripped') and
doubled repetitions of the natural details are mechanistic,
but ignores other aspects which are not artificial: 'little',
'river-gleam', 'animate', 'curves', 'golden and honey-
bee'd'. I believe the function of visual detail, repetition
and fanciful conceit is not a mechanistic device but locally
effective, incising the process of unfortunate intent visualization, an inhumane concentration on outside instead
of inside. The so-called mechanistic metaphors are all
different, and not all that mechanistic – crossbow, figure
eight, shavings, and ripped; what they have in common is

not mechanism but great precision figuring visual intentness. Non-human, instead of human, nature is contemplated; what is outside is nature and what is inside is the personal life. The non-human creaturely world is reduced and reified by an excessive aesthetic gaze finally repudiated by wise hindsight. We never know if the gaze is cause or effect of the human neglect.

The poem tells as well as shows. The representation of the things, the shift from the intent concentration on 'them' to the final recognition that they were 'less things', and the repetition of 'gaze', all make explicit the hardness and definiteness of those first natural objects and in this context, form an indictment of the inattentive human being. The showing is important, especially in a poem where we are not told much of the story. It is left incomplete, to vibrate in the imagination, but not to be completed.

In that last stanza, the exaggeratedly precise description, reinforced by equally precise analogy, and the exact repetitions are gone, and the poem revises its own form. The conclusion makes it clear that the form's purpose was to analyse the process of unimaginative scrutiny by contrasting fancy and imagination. The poem shows what Coleridge meant when he spoke of fancy being used by imagination, for instance in Shakespeare's 'Venus and Adonis'. The concluding stanza says and shows what was missing, forcing us as conclusions frequently do, to read back and make our own revision. The image of the rain-obscured window-pane wonderfully gathers together the sense of distance, error and the energy of misdirected vision.

The 1913 elegies and other later poems written about his first marriage after Emma Hardy's death revisit sacred places, especially the cluster of scenes in Cornwall associated with their meeting and courtship. Hardy paid the scenes a special mourning visit, so the images were layered in time. Sometimes the images are emphatically and elaborately presented, sometimes muted, always playing a vital part. 'At Castle Boterel', for instance, place is almost disregarded, but much more detail of place is admitted than in the romantic day. The place is felt first, physically and personally, as a place revisited: 'As I drive . . . I look behind at the fading byway', and then again, physically and personally, as the word 'fading' changes from literal to metaphorical meaning and memory takes over: 'And see on its slope. . . . Myself and a girlish form'.

Like 'After a Romantic Day', the poem turns on reticence and absence, and the speaker refuses to tell what they 'did' and what they 'talked of', a refusal which makes the place sacred, possessed, enclosed and private, a topos of inexpressibility making the large though typically qualified claim:

> But was there ever
> A time of such quality, since or before,
> In that hill's story? To one mind never.

The hill's independence has been recognized at the outset, in the reference to two visits, wet weather and the wagonette in the present and dry March weather and a chaise in the past, but it is boldly claimed as backcloth for the sentimental history and journey. After the poetry of place has been personally articulated, the hill is seen as historically and prehistorically ancient, the two backward steps briefly freeing the landscape from present and past:

> Though it has been climbed, foot-swift, foot-sore,
> By thousands more.
>
> Primaeval rocks form the road's steep border,
> And much have they faced there, first and last,
> Of the transitory in Earth's long order;

Once the perspective has been lengthened, Hardy shrinks time again, violently:

> But what they record in colour and cast
> Is – that we two passed.

This extends the first tentative claim,'To one mind', phrasing the record more largely. The poet is imagining the place as poets traditionally do, as symbolic and sympathetic, sacred to himself, but also moving beyond the personal to place it, with objectivity, in and before history. He creates two points of view, one self-centred and the other place-centred, and shuttles between the two. The space between the two is small but significant, because it deromanticizes or undermines love's hyperbole and allows the lover to entertain two views at the same time. He can enjoy and transcend self – or imagine doing so – and rationally justify the enjoyment and sense of transcendence.

The double view makes a special kind of mutuality. The poetry of place found 'At Castle Boterel' presents ecstatic association and romantic nostalgia, the rapturous claims are accompanied by sadness, because the nostalgic journey will not be repeated. Hardy admits that 'Time's rigour' has removed the substance but defiantly insists that the phantom 'Remains . . . as when that night / Saw us alight'. At the end he ingeniously allows for a melancholy acceptance of time, while retreating from the longer temporal persective:

> I look and see it there, shrinking, shrinking,
> I look back at it amid the rain
> For the very last time; for my sand is sinkng,
> And I shall traverse old love's domain
> Never again.

The phantom figure's shrinking is made a matter of spatial perspective as the speaker 'actually' moves away, though it gains a weird reality, as if it were a mere physical parting. The poem accepts time and the objectivity of place by changing the emotional subject, not by denying the imagination's claim, not undoing that bold poetry of place.

In 'Beeny Cliff' Hardy reverses the process. He imagines, admires, and enjoys the romantic association – for a space – more fully and rapturously than in any poem except'After a Journey', but finally dismisses it as vanity and fancy. He accepts time and place on its terms, not his own, in an achieved realism of the imagination, a boon of maturity. The poem spends its first three verses on the past, in a recapitulation of place as it was on one specific occasion, 'O the opal and the sapphire of that wandering western sea!', and each verse associates the natural world with the lovers's emotions. The sea colours are linked with her bright hair; the sound of gulls and waves with the lovers' laughter; then nature appears alone, in rain, and stained and sunny purpled sea, before the people appear, with no emotion specified, but 'cloaked' with the cloud.

The distinction between the two views of place, subjective and objective, becomes clearer. The sense of place is allowed to accompany and then merge with the sense of the past love, to be briefly assimilated by it but then separating from it violently at the end. Beeny Cliff is still there, so the innocent but rhetorical question arises, 'shall she and I not go there once again now March is nigh?' but the answer has to be no:

What if still in chasmal beauty looms that wild weird
    western shore,
The woman now is – elsewhere – whom the ambling
    pony bore,

And nor knows nor cares for Beeny, and will laugh
　　there nevermore.

We have had the two viewpoints, but the one succeeds
the other, they are not and cannot be held simultaneously.
There is no mention of death, only, after the pause of the
dash, the stunning euphemism, 'elsewhere', a perfect
example of Hardy's ability to sound spontaneously over-
come with emotion and also reflect on the artifice of
poetic craft: that dash shows him sensitively choosing
between words. Though the woman is vivid at the
beginning, she remains mere memory, her ghost too frail
for haunting. The place, like the woman, has been fully
rendered in its past physical beauty and animation, but in
the last two stanzas it is metonymized in the cliff, whose
massiveness and funny nickname-like name can permit an
affectionately deprecating tone, 'bulks old Beeny'. Nature
is as detached as it is in Housman's 'Tell me not here, it
needs not saying', and like Housman's enchantress is
ironically personified in order to be made distressingly
impersonal.

'After a Journey', one of the warmest and most sensuous of the elegies, begins composedly, 'Hereto I come to
view a voiceless ghost', which seems to acknowledge the
oddity of trying to make a dialogue out of soliloquy, and
to resist the popular form of dramatic monologue. There
is nothing the speaker would like as much as a reply from
the voiceless ghost, but place, sacred place, is all there is
at first. Because the place has stayed the same it stimulates
memory until the old haunts become haunted, and the
ghost is raised. The poem takes the form of a physical
invocation. The first line states the lover's intent, the
second anticipates the beloved's presence: 'Whither, O
whither, will its whim now draw me?', and three lines
later the ghost is fondly apostrophized, moved from 'it' to
'you', and can start her haunting. Hardy's invariable

'seems' is not applied to the ghostly woman, but to the sound of the waters above the cave, though an effective ambiguity blurs the non-human with the human. (The Tennyson reader is reminded of his lyric of memory, 'In the Valley of Cauteretz', in which a valley's music echoes a voice from years ago – thirty-two to Hardy's forty.) The separation of the waterfall and its voice here helps to merge place and person:

> I see what you are doing: you are leading me on
>> To the spots we knew when we haunted here
>> together,
> The waterfall, above which the mist-bow shone
>> At the then fair hour in the then fair weather,
> And the cave just under, with a voice still so hollow
>> That it seems to call out to me from forty years ago,
>>> When you were all aglow,
> And not the thin ghost that I now frailly follow!

But the ghost is not all that thin, nor the frail man entirely feeble. Though he sounds passive, he is in charge of the place, in every aspect of the scene, a deep and potent animator, a source though also a product of its poetry. This transformation is what imagination can bring about. And the woman is allowed her triumph, until dawn. She goes then not because Hardy knows ghosts are illusions but because it is when superstition banishes all ghosts. There is something like a statement of faith, as if he were resting on the tradition, which privileges and permits the final claim that the speaker has not changed but is the same as he was, put forward – surely[3] – in happy energy and intimate reassurance.

Of all the elegies, 'After a Journey' is the most sensual and seductive poem, a second-honeymoon elegy. The animal details like the preening birds and the lazily flopping seals, smoothly, softly, and shiningly tangible, all contribute to the sensuality, as does the *double entendre* of dangerous haunting and wanton allure. The grey-eyed woman with nutbrown hair is not just a ghost, but tantalizingly elusive, mobile, unpredictable, flirtatious, fleshly, 'where you will next be there's no knowing', with blood which is circulating, 'the rose-flush coming and going'. Hardy's speaker is excited: he wants to take the wax out of his ears or be untied from the mast, to abandon himself to his sea-ghost. He allows himself to be seduced, and this seduction is proved by, or permits, that relaxation of reason at the end:

> nay, bring me here again!
> I am just the same as when
>   Our days were a joy, and our paths
>   through flowers . . .

Reason is heard in the reminder of the thin ghost and the frail follower, but the curve of the lyric is the irrational rise and momentarily satisfying climax of desire, the last not possible for the truth-telling Hardy of the novel's long perspectives. We feel that the ghost of this poem is believable and her erotic enchantments strong because the language is so thrilled as he desires, succumbs and believes. Her ghostliness gives an edge to the lure, a glamour, in its original sense of magic.

The poem's uncanny but physical sexiness and its wonderfully knowing and intimate tone – 'I see what you are doing: you are leading me on' – makes you feel exactly how much Hardy got out of writing these poems. As Florence Hardy ruefully observed – and no wonder she was irked – he wrote these heartbroken poems with relish, and in this one you can see why and how. He is working up the erotic imagination, as Lawrence does in 'Look, we have come through' and Yeats in the Crazy Jane poems, but as Hardy very seldom does, except in a few of his darker narrative poems. If his sex-life was disappointing, as it may have been, he enjoyed the pleasures of imagination. Here the process is unbared, the poem self-analysing, the passion released and formed.

The strange poem 'A Dream Or No' seems to rebel against the whole idea of the elegeic sacred place: 'Some strange necromancy / But charmed me to fancy'. It discusses the power of remembered place in sceptical mood, refusing to be haunted: 'But nought of that maid from Saint-Juliot I see . . .' and 'Can she ever have been here?' Its ghost is really frail, less than a ghost, simply a dream-image, and its place fails to become symbolic and sympathetic, though in its peculiar way it leaves a margin for rationality, austerity, and a displacement of romantic imagination. Because the idea of the haunting is rejected, and the notion of the sacramental journey shrugged off, the place, as well as the idea, is dismissed, and the end is a curiously moving negation, which makes its lament for absence and creates a kind of elegy, after all. If the place is not imprinted with the image of the dead woman who lived and loved there, and seemed to invite the visit and the imaginative essay, then it might as well not exist. The failure to haunt or be haunted is as expressive of grief as a haunting, and the last stanza acts as a kind of *occupatio*, as the place is doubted but made sensuous, and its place names listed allusively and in the knowledge of their place on the real map:

> Does there even a place like Saint-Juliot exist?
> Or a Vallency Valley
> With stream and leafed alley,
> Or Beeny, or Bos with its flounce flinging mist?

The odd poem out is 'Domicilium', which respectfully, perhaps a little artfully and amusedly, bestows a Latin name on a humble house, and in a way makes more room for place – but not for the most complex and passionate poetry of place – than any of his other poems. The poem is Hardy's first, written when he was sixteen, and not published in his lifetime. It has a remarkable coolness, a fullness of objective registration. Its tranquilly moving blank verse, fullness and detail, leisurely scrutinizing and parenthetic style, obviously reminiscent of 'Tintern Abbey', or rather of its slow-paced introductory section before the lyrical narrative becomes fully personal and passionately charged. Hardy's 'seem' is already present, and so is an easy awareness of imaginative process, making room for a maker's, if not an autobiographer's, presence, in a way which is personally restrained:

> It faces west, and round the back and sides
> High beeches, bending, hang a veil of boughs,
> And sweep against the roof. Wild honeysucks
> Climb on the walls, and seem to sprout a wish
> (If we may fancy wish of trees and plants)
> To overtop the apple-trees hard by.
>
> Red roses, lilacs, variegated box
> Are there in plenty, and such hardy flowers
> As flourish best untrained.

Hardy is respecting and dignifying his birthplace, first with the grand learned Latin title and then with particularity and reticence. He is not writing a poem of childhood memory teeming with nostalgia, but keeping himself out, perhaps because he is carefully transmitting the memory of his paternal grandmother. (But he must have enjoyed those sly hardy flowers.) Halfway through the poem the narrator delegates narration, making room as an inquirer and listener for the presence of his grandmother. She is given a detached and unsentimental inset presentation, her recollected emotions are presented modestly and indirectly, concentrating on the birthplace as it was and is, in the same observant unemotional quiet-flowing Wordsworthian style as the main narrator. The cut-off history, with calm summarizing last line, avoids climax and emphasizes the act of plain description. Pride of place is given to place, twice over:

> 'Yonder garden-plots
> And orchards were uncultivated slopes
> O'ergrown with bramble-bushes, furze, and thorn:
> That road a narrow path shut in by ferns,
> Which, almost trees, obscured the passer-by.
> 'Our house stood quite alone, and those tall firs
> And beeches were not planted. Snakes and efts
> Swarmed in the summer days, and nightly bats
> Would fly about our bedrooms. Heathcroppers
> Lived on the hills, and were our only friends;
> So wild it was when first we settled here.'

Hardy's poetry of place is central in his novels too, as in Emily Brontë and D. H. Lawrence, though rare enough in the history of the novel. There is poetry of place, both self-conscious and implicit, in the cliff in *A Pair of Blue Eyes* which nearly kills Elfride and her lover Knight, the inhabited woods and gardens and fields of *Under the Greenwood Tree* and *The Woodlanders*, the primitive Egdon Heath in *The Return of the Native*, ancient Casterbridge Ring, the lush dairylands of the Frome valley and the bad land of Flintcomb Ash in *Tess*, all force-filled places and theatres of action. They are all different, all individualized, but all presented in sensuous power, attractive and occasionally unattractive, in form or colour offering or refusing pleasures for the eye, touch and ear. They invite personification. Some are scrutinized as historical and sacred places, or sites of scientific interest. They are backgrounds and symbols, with particular functions in their novels as organs to the whole, as Coleridge said of Shakespeare's characters.

Imagination may seem to be in the foreground, scrupulous honesty of imagination, with the recognition that the anthropocentric view is not inevitable. But shift the scene slightly, and we are struck by the sensuous particularity with which Hardy recreates the natural habitat. We also see the reflexivity of his art, like that of the poems but on a larger scale, that Janus-faced awareness of art and nature.

In *The Return of the Native* poetry of place is grand and subtle, and shows what can happen when a poet moves to prose fiction. Even when he personifies Egdon Heath, concentratedly in the first chapter and constantly in the rest of the novel, Hardy makes us aware of his awareness of personification as rhetoric. That beginning has led various readers to speak of the heath as a character rather than a backcloth, and it is clear that Hardy is doing something no novelist has done before, though Wordsworth and Coleridge had done it in poetry. In *Wuthering Heights*, the previous English novel to make central use of nature, the non-human animal and vegetable world is always refracted through human experience. So what happens when Hardy presents that place in the first chapter, whose title renews a wellworn body-metaphor, 'A Face on which Time makes but little Impression'? Is he trying to distinguish the place from the human body?

From the first paragraph a human viewpoint is used, but mutedly and anonymously. It is vaguely individualized, as that of 'a furze-cutter' seeing day in sky and night in earth, or of a 'thorough-going ascetic'. It is also impersonalized in phrases like 'nobody could be said to understand the heath who had not been there at such a time', or 'the eye'. Whenever metaphor or personification verges on the pathetic fallacy it is cautiously qualified, immediately or proximately, by the topos of supposition: 'was as a tent', 'an apparent tendency to gravitate together', on the part of heath and night, 'a near relation', 'seemed to rise and meet the evening gloom in pure sympathy', 'appeared slowly to awake and listen', 'seemed to await something','solitude seemed to look out of its countenance'. As he discusses the congenial tragic poetry of the heath Hardy shows that poetry, and also says that he is making poetry. He deconstructs and demystifies anthropomorphism as he alerts us to the muted, scrupulous and unromantic narrator's presence.

The characters, like the reticent narrator, bring their humanity to bear on nature. Sometimes they do this naïvely, sometimes they are sophisticatedly conscious of what they are doing. The phases of the moon, for instance, are marked through the frequently nocturnal action, almost as consistently as the movements of the sun in Homer's *Odyssey* and Joyce's *Ulysses*, and the novel's moonlit scenes are occasions for subtle poetry of place. For instance, when Eustachia and Clym meet, ten minutes into a lunar eclipse, the 'remote celestial phenomenon' having 'been pressed into sublunary service as a lover's signal' Hardy registers intense imaginative activity. It begins before the eclipse, when Clym's intent gaze is imaged by a description of the 'small' moon reflected in each of his eyes. (He is to suffer from partial blindness, though connections are left to the reader's imagination.) At the moment there is no suggestion of a case of moonstruck love. He scans the 'silvery globe', learned in the contemporary names for its moonscape and moon-marks, 'the Bay of Rainbows, the sombre Sea of Crises, the Ocean of Storms, the Lake of Dreams, the vast Walled Plains, and the wondrous Ring Mountains' imagining a lunar voyage 'through its wild scenes', but Hardy knows this is virtual reality, and realises the effort by which Clym '*almost* felt himself to be voyaging' (my italics). His motive

for contemplation is important: on his return to Egdon he
hoped to find a freedom from social necessity, but he has
been disappointed, and he meditates on the moon as a
place where 'perhaps . . . at some time or other' there
might have existed 'some world where personal ambition
was not the only recognized form of progress'. While he
dreams like Tess of a freedom from contingency, he is in
touch with the reality principle and well aware that he is
dreaming. Hardy introduces the lovers' meeting with this
ironic wisdom.

When the moon is half-eclipsed, Eustachia uses it to
signify a melancholy foreboding sense of time 'slipping,
slipping, slipping', then seizes the 'strange foreign' gold
colour cast on her lover's face as an omen that he 'should
be doing better things than this'. And Clym later descends
from his lunar imaginings of the unconditional to the
earthbound and conventional fantasy of moonlight in
Paris demanded by Eustachia's romantic ignorance, 'the
Little Trianon would suit us beautifully to live in, and
you might walk in the gardens in the moonlight . . .'. The
lovers' imaginations work very differently as they contemplate their pastoral. Like many novelists, Hardy uses the
poetry of place to mark the psychic and physical action,
but by keeping a scrupulous separation between human
nature and non-human nature, he asserts the independent
presence for the habitat. Because it is being pressed into
symbolic service by the minds and passions of its people,
its stubborn difference and independence is appreciated,
ironically and austerely brought into play. And at the same
time, the work of imagination is noticed.

Hardy shows this blend of austerity and richness when
he uses Egdon's summer heat and hardness to kill Mrs
Yeobright. The novel and some of its characters are as
aware as *King Lear* and some of its characters, that though
non-human nature hurts and kills, and can be read as a
tragic symbol, its deadly indifference is put in perspective

by man's inhumanity. The often noted resemblance to *King Lear*'s plot and imagery is clinched when Mrs Yeobright is killed by an adder's bite and Hardy transforms Lear's metaphor of the serpent's tooth for filial ingratitude into a fiction's 'real' animal. We also meet Lear's insight that only 'when the mind's free, the body's delicate', as Mrs Yeobright explains that she is not suffering from the heat, 'Ah, I am exhausted from inside'. She feels relieved by the sky and the shepherd's thyme, observes the remote bustling ants' colony, envies the heron's sunlit soaring 'in the zenith' which 'seemed a free and happy place', but longs for her son's house, on 'the earthly ball to which she was pinioned'. The poetry of place plays a part, and it is seen again as detached from the human drama, placed by the narrator and the imagination of the characters.

At the end of the novel, the green world and the human story are brought together and distinguished for the last time, on Mayday. As in many nature rituals in ths novel, including its first, the solstice bonfire, nature and human beings are joined in symbol, ceremony and tradition. Hardy moves from a sensuous account of the new delicate birch leaves and the people decking the horizontal pole with flowers, to an anthropological comment on ritual:

> Indeed, the impulses of all such outlandish hamlets are pagan still . . . homage to nature, self-adoration, frantic gaieties, fragments of Teutonic rites to divinities whose names are forgotten, seem . . . to have survived mediaeval doctrine. (Bk 6, Chap. 1)

From the idea he turns back to the individual, rendered in sensuous new detail in a scene which dramatizes the process of an awakening. Thomasin is asked by Diggory Venn, a new man in his white skin, and a green man in his flowered waistcoat and green coat, if the Maypole can be put up 'in the nice green place' outside her house, Blooms-End. She draws her curtains on Mayday morning to see the maypole 'sprung up in the night', opens the window to an air so sweet and 'free from every taint' that she tastes the fragrance on 'her lips', then observes the elaborate structure of floral arrangement. Hardy neatly makes description general and specific: at the top hooped 'small flowers', then layers of Maybloom, bluebells, cowslips, lilacs, ragged-robins, daffodils 'and so on till the lowest stage was reached'. Her May meeting with Diggory is skilfully retarded, and not until the next chapter, beautifully entitled 'Thomasin Walks In a Green Place by the Roman Road', does their old courtship begin again 'on green turf and shepherd's thyme'.

The fertility rites are doubled in a natural-seeming relaxed symbolism which is explicated pedagogically then shown alive in action. As in some of the poems, there is the imaginative construction of desire and satisfaction. The poetry of place is in forms and colours of spring's renewal, poetry about place is made by the characters as they renew primitive rites, and both kinds are made by the novel for its readers. Hardy believed that the form of a novel could give pleasure, and his rites, seasons and shapes are balanced: we began with the burnt furze of the bonfire at the winter solstice, and we end with the Maypole. The lovers tread the same shepherd's thyme observed by Mrs Yeobright as she died.

There is the sense of completion, but the novel does not end here. The love story of natives who have never left their native place is placed in history and tradition, as Clym Yeobright, the returned native, is left outside their wedding party, and the actual ending projects his fate and future, briefly returning us to the spot where the story began, then going beyond. The poetry of place expands:

he laboured incessantly in that offfice, speaking not
only in simple language on Rainbarrow and in the
hamlets round, but . . . from the steps and porticoes of
town-halls, from market-crosses, from conduits, on
esplanades and on wharves, from the parapets of
bridges, in barns and outhouses, and all other such
places in the neighbouring Wessex towns and villages.
(Bk 6, Chap. 4)

Clym Yeobright stands on Rainbarrow 'just as Eustachia had stood . . . some two years and a half before', but
the story is enlarged culturally and geographically: neither
novel nor native is contained by Egdon Heath. The last
sentence is a Shakespearean ending in which we are
alerted to the fact of fiction in a way which combines
closure and openness, of place and of narrative: 'But
everywhere he was kindly received, for the story of his
life had become generally known'.

From Rainbarrow to everywhere: Hardy is one of the
best-known regional authors, reinventing the name and
nature of Wessex, blending the real and the imaginary for
poetry of place, and writing most tenderly about alienation from homeland in one of his best war poems,
'Drummer Hodge', where he anticipates Rupert Brooke's
'The Soldier' in odd and exotic particulars of foreign place
and place names. But Hardy was an internationalist, taking
regional and local allegiance and responsibility as experience and sign of neighbourhood not patriotism. The
expansion of *The Return of the Native* is imagined in his
poems against nationalism. 'The Pity of It', written in
1915, anticipates Wilfred Owen's conclusion that the
poetry is in the pity, and quotes the soldier Othello for its
title. It starts in 'loamy Wessex lanes' and uses local dialect,
'"Thu bist", "Er war"', to urge the pity of fighting 'kin
folk kin tongued'. 'His Country', written in 1913, imagines imagination travelling to find 'all the men I looked

upon / Had heart-strings fellow-made', modifying a passionate conclusion to insist that it is imagination speaking, with the scrupulous 'seems'. It is a spare poem, with no visualization, no poetry of place:

> I traced the whole terrestrial round,
>   Homing the other side;
> Then said I, 'What is there to bound
> My denizenship? It seems I have found
>   Its scope to be world-wide.'

CHAPTER SEVEN

Sexual Imagination: The Monologues

From long experience of writing for an avid but highly shockable reading-public Hardy bitterly compared the publication of prose and poetry. His memoir *The Later Years of Thomas Hardy*, which was published as the work of his second wife, Florence Hardy, shows him speculating about subversive ideas in literature, after the publication of *Jude* in 1896:

> Perhaps I can express more fully in verse ideas and emotions which run counter to the inert crystallized opinion – hard as a rock – which the vast body of men have vested interests in supporting. To cry out in a passionate poem that (for instance) the Supreme Mover or Movers ... must be either limited in power, unknowing, or cruel ... will cause them merely a shake of the head; but to put it in argumentative prose will make them sneer, or foam, and set all the literary contortionists jumping upon me ...

He is writing here about religious subversion, but the observation also applies to his sexual realism, which was criticized as shameful and obscene by editors, reviewers, and even friends. He always insisted that his novels were not argumentative or programmatic, but after *Jude* he was forced to recognize that prose fiction was taken to be argumentative and dogmtic, in ways which poems were not.

In fact, many of his monologues and dialogues about God are more iconoclastic and scornfully critical of Christianity than the novels. Many of them are sexually subversive too, though never or hardly ever dogmatic or argumentative. As poetry is more open in its invitations to the unconscious mind, and may be less rationally scrutinizing than prose fiction, so Hardy's poetry sometimes plumbs depths which the novels seem to pass over, though sometimes with a suggestive tremor. The depth and darkness of his poetry about sex may often be missed, even by tolerant modern readers who understandably find the overtly sexual novels, a more exciting and easy read. Perhaps Hardy himself did not realize the nature of all his poetic revelations, which may have passed the private screen of self-censorship without being identified and were not subjected to a public sceening by editors.

Sexuality is not a prominent subject in the love lyrics, which are not always romantic but are hardly ever sensual. The exceptions, like 'After a Journey', smuggle in sensuousness through non-human somatic sensations, in the imagery of sea, weather or non-human animals. Sensuality is strong and central in the narrative poems in which the impersonative imagination, as Hardy liked to call it, is strongest. This powerful group of poems, ballads and monologues seems to have been overshadowed by the lyrics of nature, love and death, but they are important for a full understanding of the artist and the man, as they show Hardy's imagination working in a way which is special to their genre. If we compare them with the novels, they are even more concerned with sex, particularly with the constructions of desire. They show Hardy as a poet of the sexual imagination, like those two other great Victorian erotic poets, Swinburne and Clough.

In the novels sex is shown offstage, as in the ambiguous account of Tess's rape or seduction, Sue's sexual revulsion for Phillotson, and Jude's one-night stand with Arabella, or in symbols like Troy's sword-play in *Far From the Madding Crowd*, or in figures like the peremptory orders and the schoolmaster's arm in *Jude*, or in synecdochic events like Manston's organ-playing or Tess's milking, or in sensuous descriptions, like the muslin froth of Tess's skirt, the inside of her mouth, her mushroom-textured skin, and the rank-smelling weeds in Dairyman Crick's garden.

We are often aware of the narrator's – or behind 'him'[1] the author's – indulgent and excited sexual imagination but what is lacking in the novels is interiorized sexual fantasy. In *The Return of the Native*, for instance, Eustachia is described in voluptuous detail, but the love which Stendhal called crystallization and which Hardy analyses in Eustachia's attachment to Clym, is interestingly shown in emotional complexities, but strikingly lacking in physical desire. Even the relationship between Eustachia and Wildeve, in which Wildeve's desires are clear, is ambiguous, because of the absence of sexual detail, physical and psychological. They behave like lovers but we do not know if they have slept together, nor is her feeling for him always clear. In such a dominant character, Eustachias's sentimental history is left vague, and this has always seemed to me a weakness in a great novel. *The Well-Beloved*, whose very subject is the mobility of sexual fantasy, and the moving crystallization of desire, relies entirely on telling and evades showing, even the indirect ways of showing found in the earlier novels. What is absent from the characters in the novels, even when they are centrally concerned with desire, though not from the narration, is sexual imagination.

However, it is the pre-occupation of some of his most original poems, the first-person dramatic ballads and monologues which are both narrative and lyric: 'A Tramp-woman's Tragedy', 'The Burghers', 'Sacrilege', 'Her Death and After', 'A Face at the Casement', 'The Collector Cleans His Picture' and 'The Chapel Organist'. They are examples of his subtle and surprising use of sensuous lyric in telling a story, and their main subject is sexual passion. In each the plot is moved by a psychological insight into sex, but the story is placed and dramatized by the first-person poem. Each poem finds a form for the motive and movement of passion, and in each the actual subject is emotion and passion. They are poems which discover, explore and analyse the passions by imagining and individualizing the nature and action of sexual imagination, startlingly and often shockingly.

Like Browning in his dramatic monologues, Hardy sometimes apostrophizes a putative reader who blends with the internalized interlocutor we all address, and sometimes a more or less defined listener, as in the conversation poems. As the first-person narrators relate their sensational histories of murders, executions, lusts and treacheries, the tensions, surprises and dénouements are in the tale and the manner of telling. These narratives are what Bernard Shaw might have called unpleasant poems, and they excite, disgust, shock and frighten us by their impersonations of lust, love, jealousy, obsession, posses- siveness and cruelty. They are sensitively and analytically unpleasant, not crudely melodramatic or pornographic, though there is melodrama and pornography in some. In them Hardy scrupulously imagines the nature of the passions, their oddity and arbitrariness, their surprising motives and power, their riddling or unfathomable after- math and consequences. This is to make them sound wholly conscious, but the unconscious usually seems to play a part in the writing.

There is not always a clear dividing line between the kinetic appeal of melodrama and pornography, and dis- tanced aesthetic appeal. What is fascinating in Hardy is partly the sensational material itself, the shock and horror of the sex and violence, and also what is revealed in the particularized affective life of the characters, the uninhibi- ted compulsions of pleasure and the perversions of desire.

Each poem in the group of poems I want to discuss turns on some discovery of passion, through an individual act of imagination.

John Stuart Mill, who was read and quoted by Sue Bridehead as well as her author, insisted in his 'Essay on Poetry' (1833) that the mature art of poetry delineated the workings of emotion, as the crude and extrovert novel could not do; and though Hardy is one of many novelists who proves Mill wrong, the poems give the impression that the poem is revealing the nature of emotion and passion to the poet, as he contemplates, invents, and constructs his acts of feeling, and as he makes the affective experience impersonal and fictitious, placing it outside himself and perhaps seeing it more clearly. His gentlest, sweetest and morally admirable feelings are admissible in his personal lyrics – though Hardy insisted that they were all 'impersonative' too – but some varieties of his sexual imagination seem to have needed a fictional form.

In the tragic action of 'A Trampwoman's Tragedy', a poem which Hardy once said was his best, all the principal characters but one die an untimely death. It is the tramp-woman's tragedy because she is its protagonist and because she is its narrator. A man and woman lightly start an imaginative game which gets out of hand and eventually provokes a jealous imagination, with fatal consequences. The situation is entirely plausible but it also has a startling unreality about it, because the flirting trampwoman and jeering John have no love or desire for each other but are indeed content with their partners – at least she is – and are acting on whim, imagining infidelity, playing around in a play which becomes reality. When the trampwoman sits on John's knee to tease her lover and he asks her if he is the father of the child she is carrying, she answers, still fooling, that its father is John, parenthetically informs the reader 'God knows 'twas not', and her lover knifes him.

Before the crisis, the trajectory of feeling has been

started. It is twisted, like two interwound cords, as the first-person narrator tells solemn truths to the reader and flighty lies to her true lover. Before we get to the murder, the relationship of the two lovers is obliquely but clearly articulated. Hardy's sense of the tramps' life is solidly specified and placed in a region he knew well, where he too had travelled and walked. Their daily life is thoroughly imagined as a hard and companionable toil (like Gabriel Oak's and Bathsheba's, if less productive) and their habits of loving, enduring and travelling are figured in a list of inns, recollected affectionately and specifically by the narrator, in a tale of small endurances, a mapped routine and rooted fidelity of place:

> For months we had padded side by side,
>   Ay, side by side
> Through the Great Forest, Blackmoor wide,
>   And where the Parret ran.
> We'd faced the gusts on Mendip ridge,
> Had crossed the Yeo unhelped by bridge,
> Been stung by every Marshwood midge,
>   I and my fancy-man.
>
> Lone inns we loved, my man and I,
>   My man and I;
> 'King's Stag', 'Windwhistle' high and dry,
> 'The Horse' on Hintock Green. . . .

As is his way Hardy psychologizes his ghost story and particularizes his ghost. The dead lover compulsively repeats his mortal question in a tercet beautifully adapted to excited fluency, giving the woman a belated second chance:

> The ghost of him I'd die to kiss
> Rose up and said:'Ah, tell me this!
> Was the child mine, or was it his?'

The recognition of the whim and flimsy play that provoked deadly anguish and jealousy is made in the deadly earnest of her dramatic language, in its repetitions, its apostrophes, its grim joke, 'die to kiss', the emphatic stern ceremony of its rhyme:

> O doubt not that I told him then,
>   I told him then,
> That I had kept me from all men
>   Since we joined lips and swore.
> Whereat he smiled, and thinned away
> As the wind stirred to call up day . . .
>   – 'Tis past! And here alone I stray
>   Haunting the Western Moor.

There is a weird wry happiness when she tells him the truth and the poem modulates from living to dying as he smiles like a man then thins into a traditional ghost who must depart at dawn, a troubled spirit laid to rest. She injured him casually: casualty has a special role in Hardy because he knows how ironically powerful mere chance can be in the world without a providence, and also knows how fragile the best human relationships may be. But there is a kind of fidelity, though also a doom. The trampwoman's metaphorical haunting – alone and straying – balances and resembles her lover's real haunting. The poem's action goes into reverse as she is bound by the fidelity she once playfully injured, and the name and title take on a new significance as she seems impelled to go on tramping – and go on telling, as the repetitive form perhaps suggests? – like the Ancient Mariner.

As so often in these highly formalized narratives, conventions and crafts of style and structure are marked. Though the form is suited to impassioned speech, it is also unremittingly conspicuous, joining the verse habits and subject matter of the ballad, rooted in oral tradition, with an awareness of narrative at its least social, most guiltily isolated, and most compulsively communicative. The teller makes the imaginative story unmistakably reflexive. What Hardy's violent men and woman have in common with Henry James's sensitive fantasists is the characterized imaginative narration.

Another grim ballad of crime and punishment, with a similarly assertive narration and lyrical power is 'Sacrilege', sub-titled 'A Ballad-Tragedy'. The story of twins, it takes the form of a twinned narrative. The first speaker tells a listener, who is eventually identified as his twin brother, how the woman he loves persuades him to steal the church treasure to buy jewels and finery. He enjoins his brother to kill her if he is charged and hanged, so that she cannot go back to her old lover Wrestling Jack and trouble his spirit. It is a fascinating recognition of the rational self-possession which can co-exist with sexual abandon, and even more plainly than the final confession of 'A Trampwoman's Tragedy', a primitive enjoinder to ensure the peace of the dead, like that recognized by Antigone and Odysseus. Like the trampwoman, the sacrilegious lover tells a startling story with a subtle and unpredictable emotional trajectory. So does his brother the revenger.

We read the first half as the beginning of a conversation poem where we do not know who is addressed or if it is addressed to a particular character at all. The narrator, who seems to be the major character, may be talking to himself or addressing an impersonal reader. But the poem is constructed to twist and surprise us, though slowly. Only when we reach the last two stanzas of the first half and the first monologue, do we find that the storytelling is sternly motivated and intimately directed: 'I come to lay this charge on thee'. We do not yet know that a brother is telling and laying the charge on a brother. The characters and story take a new turn at the beginning of the second half and second monologue, as the second story-teller solemnly reveals the relationship, in two lines, 'Thus did he speak – this brother of mine. . . ./ Born at my birth of mother of mine'.

The avenger takes over the narrative with moral responsibility. He records fear, 'I kept the watch with shaking sight', baldly reports, 'They stretched him; and he died', then tells his revenge story. The subtle shift of narrator, in an assimilation of structure to psychology, is comparable to the transition in Henry James's *The Golden Bowl*, when the Prince, narrator of the first book, hands over the story-telling and action of the second book to the Princess, in an exchange of active and passive roles.

In 'The Sacrilege' a passionate event transforms lives. There is a change of emotional track as we shift from one man's passions to another and move from violent cause to violent effect. It is a sensational poem, but it uses emotional understatement: for instance, the murderer's bonding to the twin for whom he has to kill, is never mentioned but taken for granted, and the perfect unde-tected and reluctant murder smoothly follows from the first imperative. The title, as well as the narrative structure, turns out to be ironic and misleading, because the sacri-lege is not the most important crime in the story. The murderer has qualms before he pushes the woman into the water, but no conflict: the twin's promise is irresistible and leads inexorably to the murder. At the end Hardy dwells on remorse: the murderer will always see the dead woman's ropes of hair on the water, and hear her scream; but the primitive response to the brother's charge is even stronger tnan the moral ending. The fate of the twins, bonded in love-sacrifice, seems ancient and terrible, like a feud in Greek tragedy or the Norse sagas.

'The Burghers' shows a man's development in sexual jealousy, travelling considerable emotional distance in a short time. A wronged husband assumes that killing will be his revenge for infidelity: 'A moment yet / As prayer-time ere you wantons die!' but his mood and the story's focus change when he sees his wife's gaze, hears her cry of 'love illimited', recognizes a look of 'love so thorough-sped' which has never been his, and is 'Blanked by such love'. The lovers' changing emotions are also observed, and they accompany him to her room, 'as if brain and breast / Were passive'. He rouses himself from apathy, a 'sad drowse', decides to be magnanimous, looks at a mirror reflecting their beauty and his lack of it, and lets them go, endowed with rich possessions. But his jealousy has deepened, not disappeared. Beginning with a conventional cuckold's honour, he learns to imagine better, and the poem ends with telling understatement as revenger, like reader, imagines the future imaginative pain of his victims, leaving slowly, 'as in surprise'. A brief word to the burgher's conventional friend says all:

'"Fool," some will say,' I thought. – 'But who is wise,
Save God alone, to weigh my reasons why?'
– 'Hast thou struck home?' came with the bough's
    night-sighs.

It was my friend. 'I have struck well. They fly,
But carry wounds that none can cicatrize.'
– 'Not mortal?' said he. 'Lingering – worse,' said I.

Hardy revised this excellently suggestive ending: he had unfortunate second thoughts, but wiser third thoughts, when for the *Collected Poems* of 1919 he explicated and replaced 'Lingering' with 'remorseful', then reverted to the less explicit 'Lingering' in subsequent editions.[2] Once again a first-person narrator is needed to tell enough, but no more, of his inner feeling.

In 'The Face at the Casement', another man is seized by unexpected jealousy, after his betrothed takes him on

a brief visit to her rejected dying lover. As he looks back
to see a pale face at the window, he acts on an impulse
which he cannot explain:

> It was done before I knew it;
> What devil made me do it
>   I cannot tell!
>
> Yes, while he gazed above,
> I put my arm about her
> That he might see, nor doubt her
>   My plighted Love.
>
> The pale face vanished quick,
> As if blasted, from the casement,
> And my shame and self-abasement
>   Began their prick.
>
> And they prick on, ceaselessly,
> For that stab in Love's fierce fashion
> Which, unfired by lover's passion,
>   Was foreign to me.
>
> She smiled at my caress,
> But why came the soft embowment
> Of her shoulder at that moment
>   She did not guess.

Remorse and jealousy are powerfully irrational and
private, and both irrationality and privacy are told from
inside, in the first person. This poem has retrospective
action: after sharing the confession we realize that we are
excluded from the woman's point-of-view — an exclusion easier to manage in a first-person's selective story.
She has spoken suggestively from her unknown secret
life, 'He wished to — marry me', but she is innocent of

her betrothed's jealous action, taking the soft embow-
ment of her shoulder as a mere fond touch, not a staged
aggression. The poem is short and the jealous action
slight but crucial, revealing, and determining a character
and his history. The impulsive jealousy, which he feels is
outside himself and something for which he is not
responsible, is like many emotions in Hardy, endlessly
regretted and life-changing, as the end of the poem demonstrates. The tendency to be not only overwhelmed but
astonished by one's own passions is a recurring trait in
Hardy.

Though there is a remorseful stanza about the dead
man's grave, it is not the end, which is bitter generalization. It is as if the narrator is compelled to end with a
judgement which ironically reflects on cause and effect,
to imply the death of love:

> Love is long-suffering, brave,
> Sweet, prompt, precious as a jewel;
> But jealousy is cruel,
> Cruel as the grave!

The end endorses the enigmatic narrative gap: there is
no mention of the subsequent life of the betrothed couple,
and this is perfectly acceptable in a characterized first-
person act of narrative, where selection is expected and
there is no omniscience.

Hardy's ballads, like his stories, are sometimes disappointing, and can show his imagination working at a low
pitch, but even a weak poem may have its moments, in
freshly articulated and unexpected emotions. For instance,
in the early ballad 'Her Death and After', one impassioned
stanza lifts action out of the conventional track of ironic
misadventure in which a man responds to his old love's
terrible marriage-story and a wish that her lame child was
his:

– When I had left, and the swinging trees
Rang above me, as lauding her candid say,
Another was I. Her words were enough:
    Came smooth, came rough,
  I felt I could live my day.

The life-changing in this poem is unusually happy,
though the foster-father's story ends with remorse and
doubt, bluntly expressed:

    . . . I gave the child my love,
And the child loved me, and estranged us none.
But compunctions loomed; for I'd harmed the dead
    By what I said
  For the good of the living one.

One of Hardy's most compelling first-person narratives
is 'The Collector Cleans his Picture', where there is
a dynamic relationship between the surface story and
the sub-text. As the collector slowly strips his picture,
cleaning it to reveal unclean lust and disease, so the
poem uncovers, slowly and suggestively, the repressed
unconscious dark side of the conscientious clergyman
following his innocent hobby. What is unimagined forces
its way into the open, from the buried life of art and
sexuality. It has been said that the poet, scholar, clergyman and collector William Barnes was the origin of
this poem, but if Hardy intended any such allusion, in
such a powerfully ugly psychodrama, he did not fathom
the deepest meanings of his own poem. And that is
possible.

As the collector uncovers the painting, so the reader
reads the poem, also seeing what lies underneath, slow
move by slow move. In the first stanza we hear of
the blameless public life of the rural parson, busy in
duty:

Faith I was well-night broken, should have been fully
Saving for one small secret relaxation,
One that in mounting manhood had grown my hobby.

The secrecy of the relaxation seems excessive for mere
collecting and restoring, and its suggestiveness may grow,
for the modern reader, with the metaphor 'in mounting
manhood'. In *Some Versions of Pastoral* William Empson
said that all that was needed to bring out the sexual
symbolism of *Alice in Wonderland* was to retail the events,
and the same is true of this poem. The sexual appositeness
of the images are unlikely to have been intended by
Hardy, whose innocence of *double entendre* is well known:
a good example is the repetition of 'prick' in 'The Face at
the Casement'. But the poem's secret does not depend on
ambiguity or *double entendre*: the first stanza brings out
repression and need for release, the second stanza describes
the collector's new grime-covered acquisition, 'Never a
feature manifest of man's painting', and the last two
stanzas take us lubriciously, through the process of cleaning. The teller excitedly spots the telling details, bits of
female body, fair flesh, curve, and a finger significantly
pointing slantwise, and relates the supposed moment of
discovery when the priest-restorer surprisingly kisses the
supposed Venus. She is described as 'ranker', though not
as rank as the venereal under-image which is next
revealed, and which violently changes desire to repulsion:

– Then meseemed it the guise of the ranker Venus,
Named of some Astarte, of some Cotytto.
Down I knelt before it and kissed the panel,
Drunk with the lure of love's inhibited dreamings.

Perhaps with an echo of folk-tales about the ugly crone
as the inner reality of the beautiful woman, the Victorian
fear of venereal disease is clearly imaged:

Till the dawn I rubbed, when there leered up at me
A hag, that had slowly emerged from under my hands
   there,
Pointing the slanted finger towards a bosom
Eaten away of a rot from the lusts of a lifetime. . . .
– I could have ended myself at the lashing lesson!

Again, 'rubbed', 'under my hands' and 'lashing' need
no extra emphasis for a modern reader, but they are not
needed to suggest that this sexual disgust looks back to
King Lear's erotic madness, 'But to the girdle do the gods
inherit', and resembles the ruined and repulsive *Picture of
Dorian Gray*. The kiss and the knowledge of 'inhibited'
dreaming make it probable that Hardy was aware of the
poem's sinister uncovering of the id or shadow-self. The
first-person repressed clergyman necessarily tells his story
himself.

In the prefatory note to *Jude the Obscure* Hardy speaks
of sex as the strongest appetite known to man, and in this
poem he shows the dread and disgust which can attend
that appetite. Baudelaire had a short dissolute life and
Hardy a long repressed one, but they were contemporaries.

Imagining 'The Chapel Organist', however, Hardy
observes that sex may not be the strongest appetite. The
poem is another subtly sensual narrative, though it is
sometimes dismissed as a late melodramatic exercise. It is
the story of a woman who prostitutes herself in order to
make music and is driven by religious intolerance to
poison herself. Subject and form are obviously modelled
on Browning's grim crime-monologues, like 'The Lab-
oratory', but unlike the jealous heroine of that poem, the
chapel-organist reveals past, present and future to the
reader, as she meditates during her last performance.
Hardy found it necessary to explain the narrative situation

to Sydney Cockerell, who read proofs of *Late Lyrics and Earlier*:

> she is indulging in those reflections on the *last* night –
> immediately before her suicide. . . . Of course, it is all
> inferential since nobody could *know* the final thoughts
> of a woman who was dead when they found her: but
> this is a recognized licence in narrative art, though it
> should be veiled as much as possible.[3]

The dramatic monologue is a lyrical portrait of a passionate musician who – perhaps like her author – prefers her art to anything in life. There are two languages in the poem, the music played in the poem, approximately mimed by the long regular rhythmical singing lines, and the private narrative. The monologue is desperate but self-possessed enough to be critical, and a feminist irony salts the poem. The woman hears the chapel elders pruriently deplore the sexuality which is inseparable from her creative appeal as singer, player and performer – this is not made explicit but it is clearly there in the language, 'No woman's throat richer than hers!':

> 'But – too much sex in her build; fine eyes, but
>   eyelids too heavy;
> A bosom too full for her age; in her lips too
>   voluptuous a dye.'

Linked with the critical irony is her flow of defiant confessional. She dismisses sex, boldly and carelessly, shrugging off her body's charms and men's desire as a source of 'victual' while she engages in her proper business and art. She plays the chapel organ, first for poor pay then for nothing, and moves from confident scorn to despair when she is told she must give up the music which is her life. The poet finds an aptly masculine, military and sexual image for her pain and destructive shock: 'The news entered me as a sword; / I was broken . . .'.

The image of wounding is not sensationalist, because the poet has convinced us that music is her ruling passion by finding for it an apt language. She uses her technical terms knowingly and amorously, 'the psalmody notes that I love', 'those melodies chorded so richly', 'my much-beloved grand semibreves'; she ironically and appreciatively assimilates a hymn line – as her author did in 'The Impercipient' – to her Liebestod, singing 'The grave dread as little do I as my bed'. She fondly reels off a list of familiar hymn tunes, making a music of proper names, like Tamburlaine's count of conquests or the tramp-woman's list of familiar inns:

> Yet God knows, if aught He knows ever, I loved the
>   Old-Hundredth, Saint Stephen's,
> Mount Zion, New Sabbath, Miles-Lane, Holy Rest,
>   and Arabia, and Eaton . . .

It is a complex and social critical poem about a woman who has a passion for music, but we should not be too innocent about it. Like her author the chapel-organist puts her passions into her art, and shocks the public, but Hardy is not detached about his character, not entirely on her side against the chapel. The criticism of her luscious body by the voyeuristic elders is overheard by their object, to be effectively quoted and placed by her as she feels threatened, belittled and reified by their gaze. (Any implausibility about her overhearing the gossip is 'veiled' – to use Hardy's word in the letter to Cockerell – by her bitter humiliated sense of sexual reduction.) The poet savours, as he constructs, the close and morbid descriptions of a passionate desirable woman who poisons herself at the organ, drawing 'A bottle blue-coloured and fluted' from her 'round, full bosom'.

Her death, the usual death of a fallen woman, is obligatory for Victorian nemesis, but it served its author's psychic needs too. Hardy famously and lubriciously reported a woman's hanging. He imagined the erotic raptures of Manston's and Mop Ollomoor's music, and is reported to have been an ecstatic musician in his youth. Like music, poetry has many ways of serving the devices and desires of imagination, and this poem indulges the morbid need in Hardy's sexuality, as he imagines, contemplates and destroys the object of passion, who happens to be a musician. He tells his story – a Victorian 'Susannah and the Elders' – from the tragically desirable woman's point of view, but he is peeping with the chapel elders. He condemns the male gaze, but it is his.

However, he goes beyond indulgence to imagine the woman thoroughly. Like George Eliot with the Alcharisi in *Daniel Deronda*, he creates a professional artist for whom art is more important than personal relations, and lets her tell her story with complete conviction. He also imagines her imagining the men who make her their object. He can indulge but also displace sexual desire, to re-imagine sexuality in a lyrical fiction which makes the sexual woman sympathetic, sacrificial, a heroine of art. Hardy not only gazes at the woman, but gets into her mind. Perhaps it is the man's voyeurism, sexually clandestine, but controlled by art and imagined from a woman's, as well as indulged from a man's point of view, which makes the poem a disturbing sublimation but a brilliant portrait of the artist's passion.

These poems are remarkable curt narratives, and more successful, I think, than Hardy's frequently diffuse, over-compressed, prose tales. The focus on an act of life-changing imagination which concentrates character, emotion and plot, makes these ballads and monologues Hardy's best short stories, with their own way of imagining imagination, exploring new reaches of psychology, and making new versions of artistic reflexiveness.

CHAPTER EIGHT
Thresholds and Limits

INSIDE AND OUTSIDE

Hardy is an artist who imagines the limits of imagination, pushing his understanding, projection and fantasy to the verges and thresholds of creativity. Metaphors of threshold – liminal images – are frequent in his poetics of creativity, and often, unsurprisingly, take an architectural form, though we should not attach too much biographical significance to that. Images of doors, arches, windows, gateways, porches, interiors and exteriors were used by many other writers who were not architects: Donne, Herbert, George Eliot, Henry James and D. H. Lawrence, who all had the usual experience of dwellings and other buildings. Entrances and exits, doors, passages, windows, walls, fences and gates are common conveniences of vision deriving from common experiences of space and enclosure and they are all used as symbolic conveniences as artists imagine and re-imagine the trials, successes, failures and revisions of imagination.

Hardy's poetry is much occupied with what Matthew Arnold called the dialogue of the mind with itself. He meditates on the distinction and communication between the inner and outer life, important to the artist reflecting on creative solitude, and the self, and especially congenial to a thinker speculating about the conditionings of a pure or free, purer or freer, self, in social and public experience. An early poem, 'At a Seaside Town in 1869. A Lover's Reverie', dramatizes the traffic between the private and public worlds in which what we call the self forms itself, develops, changes and dies. It is not a poem where language is striking, but it is not negligible, using movement and structure originally and expressively, to create a to-ing and fro-ing, a crossing and recrossing, as a gradual process of undesirable socializing or extroversion. The poem dramatizes a kind of social and psychic osmosis in which the flow through the tissues is a two-way action and consequence, weakening the inner and strengthening the outer self.

The distinction sometimes seems blurred; it is not imagined as clear-cut. The poet images the self as interior, or as inhabiting an interior space, and society is animated as public relationships and pastimes in an exterior space which is sometimes man-made and sometimes natural: there is not a moral or psychological distinction between the natural and the artificial. What is most important in the poem's strong sense of threshold is the image of a dividing barrier, which can be crossed. This is an abstract account of what is far from abstract, because the poem tells a love story, as well as making a model of creativity.

The love story is a simple narrative, but a far from simple way of imaging imagination, and its vulnerability. In some ways it works with abstraction, constructing its story by movements in space. It focuses on the making of images, in a laconic style, mobilizing them in an incremental form in which more and more space is given to the public action, and less and less to the private. At first the privacy is an honoured and cherished space, then there is various action in and out of that space, until at the end it is lamented as a vacated sanctuary. At first there is an evenly divided occupation, as four stanzas symmetrically divide the activity of the self:

> I went and stood outside myself,
>   Spelled the dark sky

And ship-lights nigh,
And grumbling winds that passed thereby.

Then next inside myself I looked,
    And there, above
    All, shone my Love,
That nothing matched the image of.

Beyond myself again I ranged;
    And saw the free
    Life by the sea,
And folk indifferent to me.

O 'twas a charm to draw within
    Thereafter, where
    But she was; care
For one thing only, her hid there!

In the first two stanzas the imaged preference is clear as
'shone' is set against 'dark', but in the third there is a
slight tilting away from innerness with the epithet 'free',
qualified by 'indifferent', though all the explicit judgement is on the side of the inner life, which is matchless,
alluring, solicitous, and preferred to the indifferent folk.
But here is a sense of active but free and easy traffic, both
ways: 'went and stood', 'Beyond myself again I ranged',
'O 'twas a charm to draw within'.

Then in the fifth stanza we get a suggestion of a more
passive and involuntary movement from inner to outer
life, 'But so it chanced, without myself / I had to look'.
With the compulsion comes a longer span of extroversion,
'And then I took / More heed of what I had long
forsook', and the 'forsook' is the first word of divided
loyalty and attachment to the outside world. Formal
proportions endorse and demonstrate the shift, as three

stanzas are devoted to the public life, whose desirability increases, though slowly, even reluctantly. Neutral images of 'boats, the sands, the esplanade', are followed by 'the laughing crowd', and 'Light-hearted, loud / Greetings from some not ill-endowed,' where understatement conveniently marks a transition to genial social life while quietly reserving value. Charm is no longer the preserve of the private life and communication; culture and health are located in the public world where company, art and nature join in welcome and allure:

> The evening sunlit cliffs, the talk,
> Hailings and halts,
> The keen sea-salts,
> The band, the Morgenblätter Waltz.

Next, the ration of private contemplation is reduced and the ambiguity of that earlier 'hid' are brought out: 'Still. . . ./ Forward she came,/ Sad, but the same . . .'. This is an unlit appearance, and 'at night' shows a night neutrally presented, so that any amorous associations are balanced or modified by suggestions of sleep and diminished energy. After this the next public return shows the speaker more passive, and the external forces clearly and competitively amorous, – 'as by force, / Outwardly wooed / By contacts crude': exteriority is denigrated as it is empowered. Then there is a return to the structural balance at the start, the next stanza showing a decision to move back, from 'This outside life' to 'the pure / Thought-world'. The generalization of allegory declares itself but creativity is sensual as well as intellectual, the thought-world imagined in a fine oxymoron as a basking in 'her allure'. The end devotes three stanzas, including the one just quoted, to the preferred innerness, to balance the earlier three which register the takeover by exteriority. The conclusion is one of absence and loss:

the return to self is enfeebled, 'Myself again I crept within', the verb 'crept' marking a change from that first smooth entry and access; and images of privacy, seclusion and light returning to be negated. The seeker scans 'The temple where / She'd shone' but can not 'find her there' and the last stanza inexorably repeats and doubles the repetitions of effort and loss, 'sought and sought', but 'is gone, is gone'.

The poem can be read as a tragic love story but love here is a part which stands for a whole, and the imagery of passage, barrier and interaction have larger implications. The poem is about reverie and is a reverie, contemplating and enacting the strength and weakening of image-making as Hardy sees it at work in love and art, likeYeats, though less systematically and analytically. This conspicuously structured and abstractly entitled poem is also in its quiet curt way a version of the psychological dramas of division in Robert Louis Stevenson's *Strange Case of Dr Jekyll and Mr Hyde* and Oscar Wilde's *Picture of Dorian Gray*. These novels also use liminal imagery to show the divided self but with a clear and definite ethical emphasis. Hardy's poem has ethical nuances but is about the psychology of creation, its privacy and its inhibitions, and it applies to love and art, because both involve the imaginative transformation of given materials. It has even larger implications too, if we see its application to the process of acculturation and social conditioning, a dream of freedom or essence, a possible escape only in fantasy and art. My analysis makes the poem sound more abstract than it is when we relax into reading: it is a lucid paradigm for Hardy's varied and sustained meditations on imagination, but it is also a sad little lyric about love, no doubt with autobiographical roots.

A similarly constructed poem about nature, 'Self-Unconscious' also uses naïveté as a cover for subtle and complex imaginative action. Another abstract title offers a coinage to stand beside the now indispensable but then newer 'self-conscious'. Self-unconsciousness has been thought a creative advantage, even a prerequisite – for instance, by Keats and Hazlitt – but not in this poem. Once more Hardy constructs a divided action, a movement towards the threshold of vision, though the barrier between proper vision and the expense of mind in a waste of fantasy – or what seems waste – is never crossed. It is an obstacle and a limit, only retrospectively recognized as passable. Here the outer world – of nature, not society – is imaged in sparkling naturalistic detail of colour, movement and energy, used by Hardy to imagine a perilously neglected imperative, the solicitation of the outside world of natural dynamism:

> Bright yellow hammers
> Made mirthful clamours,
> And billed long straws with a bustling air,
> And bearing their load
> Flew up the road
> That he followed, alone, without interest there.
>
> From bank to ground
> And over and round
> They sidled along the adjoining hedge;
> Sometimes to the gutter
> Their yellow flutter
> Would dip from the nearest slatestone ledge.
>
> The smooth sea-line,
> With a metal shine,
> And flashes of white, and a sail thereon,
> He would also descry
> With a half-wrapt eye
> Between the projects he mused upon.

In this story thresholds are compounded, made of many things. The mind is temporarily cut off from both the phenomenal world of nature and the proper apprehension of self, by a busy distracted preoccupation with plans, projects and fantasies. These are over-externalized. The threshold uncrossed is the one which separates the sense of time, in the present, from the anticipation of time, in the future, both remembered in writing time as time past. Creativity is active, indeed it 'limns' reverie, but it is condemned for ignoring the live moment, the elusive present tense, which Hardy sees as uttering a sense of wholeness and existence. Creativity itself is imaged as interestingly rootless, suspended between inner and outer awareness. The brilliance of the outer world, presented to the reader, as to the writer's memory, condemns the inattentiveness. I think it would be a pity to make too much of the poem's real-life origins – the poem's location is said to be 'Near Bosinney' – because the particular occasion could blind us, like the distracted character in the poem, to the larger meanings, the only ones which are made specific.

The poem suggests a familiar but neglected subject, the power of that transient present moment, toasted by Horace and Herrick, understood and honoured by Hardy's admirer and successor, D. H. Lawrence, whose poetry trusts the glimpse of momentary manifestation, true to affect, spontaneous, unselfconscious, and sensuously alert. Perhaps the title of Hardy's poem suggests that to be self-conscious is to lose proper consciousness of self. Certainly he sees the unself-conscious response to immediate experience as on occasion necessary to imagination. He uses a short lyrical narrative to utter and analyse psychic experience, and make it strange. He can conceive of fantasy, usually considered part or agent of imagination, as less creative than a wise passiveness, which responds to nature's springtime creativity – 'Earth's artistries' – in a moment, catching wholeness as Hopkins catches inscape. If there is the pressure of autobiography behind the poem's considerable narrative reserve, that reserve allows an emphasis on 'clear-eyed distance' and a 'conning' of the potential experience, that would have seen 'A thing . . . / That loomed with an immortal mien'.

Like many of Hardy's poems it depends on incisive visualization. Its imaging, however, is very different from the hard-edged clear-coloured landscape in Coleridge's 'Dejection: An Ode', which figures an unbalanced heartless seeing – 'I see, not feel, how beautiful they are' – product of a disturbed imagination, a deflection of the force which brings 'the whole soul of man into activity'. Though Hardy sometimes presses with Coleridgean – and indeed Wordsworthian – power and meanings, on visual excess, as in 'Overlooking the River Stour', in the 'Self-Unconscious' the sharp visualization acts quite differently. It works from a point of view which is only imagined, not available in the past, a negative capability which responds fully to the world outside the self, and also to the self lost in reverie. The missed moment – imaginatively and oxymoronically retrieved by the poem – is defined through images of the outside world, the elated building of the yellowhammers, luminous sea and sail, with interiority characteristically and functionally left undefined, with much more than mere shyness: 'that self / As he was, and should have been shown, that day'.

The imagery of perspective, seeing at a distance and seeing whole, involves a space between the seer and the thing seen. There is also an image of seeing 'into', 'to see therein', a true *Einempfindung*. The apparently simple poem suggests a barrier between whole vision at a particular moment, and a biassed inattentive future-oriented blind creativity. No simple opposition here between inside and outside, as in 'At a Seaside Town', though this poem also uses inside–outside imagery to discover and imply imaginative power. It also surprisingly shows that the past whole vision was somehow working all the time, and can be recovered. Hardy is engaged on a search for lost time, every bit as zealously as Proust, in the tiny compass of this nature lyric.

The poem's action offers a holistic knowledge to the reader, by the strong spring of a denial and renewal. We are forced into a close and whole attentiveness to what had been ignored, the bird and sea images. We are also made to read the generalized vague language of wasted and wasting creativity, dully abstract, 'shapes that reverie limns', 'projects that he mused upon', and 'specious plans that came to his call'. The poems turns out to be a most teasing construction, because what is told to the reader is less than what is not told, and the vision which might have been, and was not, is left unspecified. The reader is placed on the ignorant side of a narrative threshold, denied access to wholeness, fed with the brilliant specificities of the non-human phenomenal world and offered nothing else. Like the 'I' in the poem, the reader also misses revelation. Like the mind of the poem which looks back in hindsight, the reader hears of – perhaps is shown? – 'that self / he was, and should have been shown, that day'. We know something big was missed but not what it was. So it is a poem about limits of vision for the reader too. In 'A Seaside Town' we are also given overspecific images of an exteriority which destroyed interiority, but given only the images, with no implications of character, history or moral interpretation, as we are in this complex poem, which deals in its small compass with subjects which occupy several books of *The Prelude* and *A la Recherche du Temps Perdu*.

Hardy's poetry about thresholds and limits is truly about itself, as it creates an active and thwarted response for its reader. It constructs a variety of invitations or temptations:

to press questioning against the barrier set up by the poem, to transgress in crossing it, (as pedantically biographical critics do, treating the poem that does not tell and name exactly like the one that does), to refuse to question, to imagine a crossing but retreat, deciding that the territory beyond is alien, no sooner sensed than denied. The last response is the most likely for the informed but critically discriminating reader, who accepts biography but measures its threshold of relevance, who respects reticence and its rewards of resonance. The poem creates a category of trespass, fencing off and forbidding traffic across boundaries, though limits may mimic thresholds, then reveal their character.

Hardy liked to imagine his own ghost, crossing the barrier between life and death. He usually does so playfully, though his play is often wry, and he most strikingly imagines life after his death not as survival but as other people's memory. For example, the elegiac imagination has seldom been imaged with more tact and reserve than in 'Afterwards'. It is a self-elegy, as modest as possible, and involves taking a step beyond the present self:

When the Present has latched its postern behind my
     tremulous stay,
   And the May month flaps its glad green leaves like
     wings,
   Delicate-filmed as new-spun silk, will the neighbours
     say,
   'He was a man who used to notice such things'?

That image of the gate is like everything in the poem, gentle and soft, the postern latched as if going were as tremulous as staying. 'Tremulous' is a word which works hard, conveying both the beats of being, as Hardy phrased it in 'The Dead Man Walking', and their fragile brevity. The controlled sibilants and the metaphor of latching create an unobtrusive and modest exit, leaving the scene without fuss or disturbance while generously welcoming the cheerful May whose young leaves are appropriately delicate and fragile. Hardy writes about life and about leaving life, bestowing the utmost tenderness on the natural world while also suggesting solicitude for his own modestly imagined memorial. (He is not always modest about this: in 'A Poet' he speaks of a dead poet beloved by 'two bright-souled women', but 'Afterwards' is a far cry from this naïve sultanlike proposal.) Its speaker is treating a difficult subject, however, as he speculates on the touchy subject of personal posthumous praise. One of his solutions is to leave out the expected obituary. This anticipation of becoming a memory is marked by the conspicuous absence of any mention of what Thomas Hardy was and is remembered for – his writing.

The poet leaves out his poetry. The teller leaves out his tales. But in doing he creates an absence which is noticeable, which draws attention to itself, and so is filled. As we read the poem we are likely to notice what it did not anticipate us remembering him for – and here the 'us' stands both for those who knew and those who did not know him. We are also likely to look for traces of the expected desire, and to contemplate those modest natural images afresh, absence desiring and becoming presence in a delicate sly transformation. The images of the poem belong to a perception of the natural world, but may also take Hardy's reader back to his poetry and novels:

> If it be in the dusk when, like an eyelid's soundless
> > blink,
> > The dewfall-hawk comes crossing the shades to
> > > alight
> Upon the wind-warped upland thorn, a gazer may
> > think,
> > 'To him this must have been a familiar sight'.

If I pass during some nocturnal blackness, mothy and
    warm,
  When the hedgehog travels furtively over the lawn,
One may say, 'He strove that such innocent creatures
    should come to no harm,
  But he could do nothing for them; and now he is
    gone'.

If, when hearing that I have been stilled at last, they
    stand at the door,
  Watching the full-starred heavens that winter sees,
Will this thought rise on those who will meet my face
    no more,
  'He was one who had an eye for such mysteries'?

And will any say when my bell of quittance is heard in
    the gloom,
  And a crossing breeze cuts a pause in its outrollings,
Till they swell again, as they were a new bell's boom,
  'He hears it not now, but used to notice such
    things'?

The new leaves, the flying hawk, the small mammal,
stars, skies and bells are all images active in his writing,
though belonging to many observant country dwellers'
experience. The imagined moderate praise comes from
acquaintances and neighbours, but can fit the experience
of strangers and readers too: 'He was a man who used
to . . .', 'To him this must have been'. . . .'He strove . . .
could do but little'. The 'eye for such mysteries' is a
testimony to his yearnings and recognitions of limits,
too. Of course it is not necessary to see these images
as artistically reflexive, but once we think of it, they
are, recalling such episodes as the wonderful Mayday at
the end of *The Return of the Native*, the starry nights
when Gabriel Oak watches his flocks, Marty's wood-

lands, Jude's pity for the birds, and Tess's fellow-feelings for trees and animals, and the sound of many bells. The images modestly generalize and assert typicality, in 'such things', but the old familiar Hardy images are being made new, in the poem. Phenomena are perceived very closely, with soft-fingered gentle delicacy, 'delicate-filmed', 'like an eyelid's soundless blink', 'mothy', and by seasoned observation and routines, 'the dewfall hawk' . . . and 'The wind-warped upland thorn', the wonderfully observed breeze cutting 'a pause' in the bell's toll and loving apprehensive sympathy with small creatures, for the hedgehog travelling furtively. Like the mysteries, the specific details are appropriate, and the projected hesitant memorial compounds the good habits of elegiac and funereal recapitulation. Hardy is writing his own elegy, with extraordinary but effective tact and understatement, and also making it psychologically exact, alert and healthy by its wondering and self-cheering tone. The ego's anticipation implies, 'What will they say?' and answers, 'Perhaps it won't be too bad: at least they might say this.' It is significantly much less morbid than many of his poems about staying alive. To meditate an elegy for his own passage summoned up the desires and wrung recognitions of a lifetime, but also gave some relief.

The well-known poem, with another abstract title, 'The Self-Unseeing', suggests imaginative loss but also sees it as an impulse to new retrieval:

> Here is the ancient floor,
> Footworn and hollowed and thin,
> Here was the former door
> Where the dead feet walked in.
>
> She sat here in her chair,
> Smiling into the fire;

> He who played stood there,
> Bowing it higher and higher.
>
> Childlike, I danced in a dream;
> Blessings emblazoned that day;
> Everything glowed with a gleam;
> Yet we were looking away!

The child dancing in a dream is recognized by hindsight; the image of blessings that emblazoned judged by
nostalgia; the gleam with which everything glowed was
not part of the remembered pleasure of smiling, fiddling
and dancing, but memory's creative vision of what was
not – and hardly ever is – sensed in the past when past
was the present. Exceptionally, one may grasp a future
memory of a present happiness, but we are nearly always
looking away. But there is in this poem a newly accrued
creative impulse, a gain of distances, which grasps the
significance which would have been incompatible with
the past creative unselfconscious joy.

Like many of Hardy's poems, this one produces an
extra image of threshold and limit, a signature of the
complex theme which is the kernel of the poem. It is not
just about the past, but about the past which was there,
or not there, for the remembered child's present. The
poem begins with a reminder of that past beyond the past
that memory is concentrating on, in that 'former' door,
already closed up in the past, and in the walking dead
feet, representing anterior pastness and retrieval, crossing
that old threshold and unobtrusively remarked by the
wonderfully suggestive footworn hollowed floor. The first
stanza is a miniaturization of the poem's central act of
memory, the part standing for the whole and also giving
the impression of a continuity and chain of memories.
The threshold between looking and looking away is a
creative facility: some joys are not compatible with what

Hardy elsewhere calls a long perspective, some visions must be retrospective. The threshold within the poem is literal and metonymic.

The articulation of a threshold between lived experience and read experience is made by the attentive reader, who is given two points of view and invited – or impelled – to move between them and make the connection which the poem does not utter and seems to deny, 'Yet we were looking away'. Crossing this threshold we temporarily convert the 'Yet' into a 'Because', but understand why the 'because' could not be in the poem. It is written within nostalgia's limits but in a way which recognizes them. There is no Proustian sense of loss but there is a Proustian sense of creative recovery, marked in the boundary between the characters – including the narrator – in the poem and the poem. There is a difference between the gains of memory imagined by Hardy and Proust: Hardy knows past experience cannot be exactly or wholly retrieved, as Proust seems to believe, though it can be made different, new, enlarged and richer. He is with Proust in revealing how the creations of memory are acts of imagination.

HUMAN BEINGS AND OTHERS

In 'Self-Unconscious' the particular figuration of nature represents animal, mineral and vegetable individualities as they can be perceived by the attentive human senses, neither coldly nor anthropomorphically but in creaturely companionship. Perhaps companionship is not a safe word: Hardy sees the nest-building birds, the sunny sea and the journeying sail as exhilarated, springlike, but separate. He does not say so, but there is a sense that the missed moment, long ago, was an experience of youth. Hardy writes many poems which mark, define and respect the boundary between human and non-human nature, focusing comprehensively on the natural world. His site for imagination, as he imagines its work, is often located on the verge of the inhuman phenomenal world. But it is a threshold usually uncrossed. In spite of his compassion for this other world, he does not usually imagine on behalf of flora or even fauna. When he does, as in 'Are You Digging On My Grave?', he uses speech to present a cool animal neutrality and to put down, decisively, the sentimental hope of fidelity from pets. Hardy does not impute human or even humanlike passion and mind to other species.

'An August Midnight' is one of many poems in which he is warm towards animal characters, but in a way which respects their distinct vitality and which, though tempted, refuses to cross the barrier between human and non-human experience. As I have already suggested, the poem creates a highly civilized human image of theatre, in which some parts are taken by the apparently humble *dramatis personae*. The stage is a page, on which almost halfway through the poem a fly is discovered rubbing its hands ('mid my page') and is joined by the rest of the cast. The human presence is confirmed as that of a writer, asserting a sense of mixed company:

> Thus meet we five, in this still place,
> At this point of time, at this point in space.
> – My guests besmear my new-penned line,
> Or bang at the lamp and fall supine.
> 'God's humblest, they!' I muse. Yet why?
> They know Earth-secrets that know not I.

It is a poem which creates a full and whole apprehension of a moment. The theatrical images, the incantatory beating clock and the repetition 'in this still place / At this point of time, at this point in space', work to concentrate the attention of the speaker in the poem and

the reader of the poem. The three 'thises' make the page
not only the page of pen and ink manuscript but also the
printed text, more obliquely and ambiguously but also
more accurately than Ted Hughes in 'The Thought Fox'
when he ends. (It is strictly speaking not true that the
'page is printed' as Hughes's speaker says, when he says it,
but Hardy's 'thises' refer to the writer's time and space, as
well as remind the reader, as Hughes does, of reading and
space.)

On this occasion the poet has his reverie about the
inferiority of the insects, but revises it. A sense of quaint
companionship patronizes the 'humblest' creatures, placing them low on the usual scale of being, affectionately,
compassionately, but hierarchically. The word 'muse',
which implies inspiration, thought and openness, seems
to make the human being retract his categories and admit
the limits of his knowledge, but he has made a start with
the hospitable image, 'my guests'. On one side of a natural
division lie his acts of mind, on the other the animals'
mystery. Of course he is struck by the difference between
what he is doing with the page and what the animals are
doing on it. But he is then struck by the opposite, too,
by the conjunction of their activities, 'Thus meet we five';
and also perhaps, subtextually, as one or two of them –
the number is not stated – die so quickly, by their
common mortality. So he is moved to acknowledge an
equality of life and to open his mind to separateness, in a
fresh and imaginative way: 'They know Earth-secrets that
know not I'.

Someone was shocked because Hardy did not know
the names of flowers (though he did know a few) but he
knew something more important, how to regard the non-
human world with intentness, respect and fellow-feeling.
He honours the space between the human being and its
creature-visitors, celebrating the limits of imagination,
hospitably allowing the insects to come into the poem on

the page after they have come on to the page in the story of the poem. If the new-penned line was a poem, it is revised, like his opinion of the animal troupe. Their antics take over the poem. They collaborate randomly, but not frivolously. They smear his ink, and he respects the death of – apparently – one of them, while recording it matter-of-factly, not elegiacally, as a banging into the light that illumines his page, to make the poem – almost – write itself. It most originally marks the distinct individuality of the human and non-human animals, in a deep heartfelt joke about sentimentality, even about romanticism. I am tempted to call it a love poem, but the point is that it is not.

Another poem which respects the difference between the human and the non-human – and again, deep beneath the difference, their common mortality – is a more direct confrontation with the romantic projection, the musing 'Shelley's Skylark'. Shelley's skylark enters the poem in two forms: as an image in Shelley's poem and as a surviving morsel of matter. To repeat, the poem can't be read without going back to Shelley's 'The Sky-lark', either in memory or re-reading. As with Tennyson's 'Mariana' it enters into a dialogue with another text, publicizing it, but here also revising. Hardy disagrees with the famous apostrophe, 'Bird thou never wert' insisting with brilliant commonsense that Shelley's skylark must indeed have been a physical individual. Hardy imagines, and makes us imagine, the bird as Shelley did not, as a real bird that lived and died, whose body was chemically recycled.

> Somewhere afield here something lies
> In Earth's oblivious eyeless trust
> That moved a poet to prophecies –
> A pinch of unseen, unguarded dust.

The dust of the lark that Shelley heard,
And made immortal through times to be; –
Though it only lived like another bird,
And knew not its immortality.

Lived its meek life; then, one day, fell –
A little ball of feather and bone;
And how it perished, when piped farewell,
And where it wastes, are alike unknown.

Bird into symbol and back into bird. Shelley's skylark, recycled in Hardy's poem, is like those insects landing on the stage-page who did not know they were getting into a poem, whose lives are identified as too inhuman for them to get in, except by the admission of alien status. He uses it and coolly insists on the uncrossable threshold between the human and the non-human creature. He does it the more powerfully because Shelley so exuberantly provided the provocation, denying the limits in order to make the bird into spirit and symbol. The romantic poet's metaphysics and mystification provokes the unromantic poet's matter-of-fact and demystifying imagination, but Hardy asserts limits and difference with such subtle restraint that readers do not seem to have grasped the sheer revisionary cheek and humour of the poem. He does not directly criticize but counters the original and originating poem with his commentary and his praise of bird and poet. It is a backhanded compliment, but still a compliment. Shelley magnificently makes Hardy imagine that his lark had once lived, so of course also died – whatever Shelley hyperbolically, ecstatically and mistakenly asserts in 'Bird thou never wert!'. Hardy makes us re-read Shelley and re-imagine his skylark more physically and completely. In the process he takes the poem further, and simply imagines the immortality 'in times to be', and rest 'in earth's oblivious . . . trust'. His cold passion perhaps inspired the sensational precision with which Ted Hughes imagines his 'Death of the Hawk'.

He takes the poem beyond dialogue, to make something new and strange. As in 'An August Midnight' we catch him in the very act of taking off for imaginative flight. There it was made conspicuous by generous self-revision, here by the generous and grateful revision of another poem and another poet, and in each case, there is a crossing of the threshold, a move from imaginative limit to a further stretch of sympathy or understanding for felt alien experience.

Hardy's animal characters are imagined, as far as animal life can be imagined. The bird poem 'Birds at Winter Nightfall' teems with tender humours, as Hardy speaks – sings, rather – like a bird:

> Around the house the flakes fly faster,
> And all the berries now are gone
> From holly and cotoneaster
> Around the house. The flakes fly! – faster
> Shutting indoors that crumb-outcaster
> We used to see upon the lawn
> Around the house. The flakes fly faster,
> And all the berries now are gone!

Witty, affectionate, fanciful, it is the bird's eye view, but imagines its other senses too, while not attempting to cross the threshold into its life. The bird is cleverly imagined simplifying the human being, as the merely instrumental crumb-outcaster, not a bad providence, less dignified and more reliable than most, marvellously recreated in the bird's nonce act of naming, and rhymed with a horticultural mouthful. Hardy uses the triolet elegantly, varying the repeated lines with great skill, and his invariable ear and eye for run-over and end-stopped lines.

There is something delicately amusing, odd and apt in representing birdsong by this sophisticated thirteenth-century French form, small-scale, repetitive, fixed and varied, and intricate metric. It draws a firm line, to remind us of difference, but also of a common hunger, cold and music.

The firm line of limit plays a more ambitious part in 'The Darkling Thrush', Hardy's most imaginative bird lyric, already discussed as a reflexive poem. It is also a poem about sympathetic nature which almost but not quite reaches beyond rational limit. The aged gauntness of the thrush and his brave unseasonal song are used expressively to convey wintriness and energy, elderly gloom and a kind of hope. The poem begins with an exaggeratedly wintry setting in which everything is reduced, grey frost, bare stems, day's eye weakened, human beings both absent and ghostlike, has a second stanza in which the century's corpse is a central image, and a last stanza in which the thrush starts up in 'full-hearted evensong / Of joy illimited', only then brought into accord with the scene's austerity, by being aged, frail, gaunt, small and 'In blast-beruffled plume'. He belongs and does not belong to the dreary scene:

> So little cause for carolings
>   Of such ecstatic sound
> Was written on terrestrial things
>   Afar or nigh around,
> That I could think there trembled through
>   His happy goodnight air
> Some blessed Hope, whereof he knew
>   And I was unaware.

It is with the greatest tentativeness that Hardy makes as if to move over the threshold dividing human from other nature, but it is only a gesture of crossing, and he hangs on to things as they are. The thrush's scrawniness is particularized, asserting a physical presence which gives good cover for symbolism, but appearances are preserved, the threshold is not crossed, animal privacy is not penetrated. The human imagination is trying its best – if best is the word – to press against limits of perception and invoke sympathetic nature but Hardy's appreciative and scrupulous recognition of the bird's separateness and difference, stays on the agnostic side of nature's division.

The poet keeps the categories intact and articulates only the possibility of taking the bird as a symbol of optimism. 'Some blessed Hope' is capitalized, and imagined lovingly, but its pressure of wish-fufilment is made clear. This is longing, candidly vague, needy, and tentative. Hope's blessed presence is permitted by the reservation, 'I could think', by the assertion that the creature's affective life – Earth's secret – must stay a mystery. So must the future and the metaphysical meanings. The poem suggests the imaginative limits of that meliorism which Hardy like George Eliot declared to be his stance, and which recognizes speculative limits. The tremor of anthropomorphism reinforces the tremulous cosmic hope but keeps it in its place. The poem imagines a pressure – the very teleological and Christian pressure Hardy resisted – to be too humanly imaginative about birds' song, so traditionally tempting to poets. If we hear a subdued dialogue with the 'Ode to the Nightingale' ('Darkling, I listen' and 'full-throated ease' behind 'full-hearted joy') it is to remember how that romantic flight touches earth to question its own symbolism, interrogating limit and threshold in ways Hardy would have found congenially scrupulous, 'Fled is that music . . . Do I wake or sleep?'

One of Hardy's most fascinating nature poems succeeds in separating the human from the non-human animal. 'The Fallow Deer at the Lonely House' first presents the deer looking through the window and then the undiscerning people looking at the fire. It is a simple, much anthologized and mysterious poem, in which once again he invokes an animal presence but does not presume to imagine it. Of course in a way he does, and the poem turns out to be a curious form of *occupatio*, in which he is writing a poem about not seeing the animal which is seen in the poem, rather as Sue imaginatively reflects the sunset for Phillotson in a mirror. It works as a poem which presents an image of nature and keeps it intact. Like many of Hardy's poems, it is much more original and innovative than it has been given credit for, or indeed than it seems on first reading:

> One without looks in to-night
>   Through the curtain-chink
> From the sheet of glistening white;
> One without looks in tonight
>   As we sit and think
>   By the fender-brink.
>
> We do not discern those eyes
>   Watching in the snow;
> Lit by lamps of rosy dyes
> We do not discern those eyes
>   Wondering, aglow,
>   Fourfooted, tiptoe.

The poem is strange in its doubled and suspended viewpoint, which dissociates the deer from the 'we'. The animal is sensitively unnamed, except in the specifying title, which stands slightly outside the poem's action, in which the impersonal pronoun 'One', making one of its most dignified appearances, presents singularity, solitude, and mystery. (It also avoids repeating 'deer' and categorizing the unseen creature by unnecessary gender.) It is also strange at the end that Hardy, a careful grammarian, flouts grammar as he moves from the two adjectives which describe the eyes, after a comma, to the two which describe the whole animal. The poem, in Hardy's curt style, is only twelve lines long and four are repetitions, and the poem is a statement about looking in and seeing, and not looking out and not seeing. But the animal is present, though description is minimal: fourfooted, tiptoe, and with glowing eyes. But the poet is imagining the deer's situation: it is given a sense of wonder, a permissible attribute in the circumstances, and there is a quiet understanding about it approaching the house, because of the snow and the light. As in 'An August Midnight', the scene-setting is reduced, and the rosy lamps are permitted, as attraction, because of their contrast with the glowing eyes in a poem which is all contrast, and perhaps as an additional barrier to human vision. The unhuman animal and the human animal are juxtaposed, like the roses inside and the snow outside in Macneice's 'Snow'. So near and yet so far: there is more than glass between the deer and the people by the fire.

THE SUPERNATURAL

An agnostic poet, Hardy constantly images the spiritual world[1] but its presence in his poetry is proposed as something imagined, not asserted as something believed. His passionate inclination keeps faith with his disbelief. As he asserts in that bitter brilliant parody of a hymn 'The Impercipient', disbelief is not caused by ignorance of belief's advantage. This unbelieving poet sometimes writes from a feeling for a supernatural object of desire, though this is more likely to be a ghost than a god. In his lyrics Hardy also records the phenomenology of disbelief, explicating his lack of faith almost as flexibly as George Herbert dramatizing varieties of religious experience. Hardy did not always write at the imaginative pitch of 'The Impercipient' and many of his dialogues with God and monologues of God are stridently polemical, but his best poetry of noumenal imagination is not only in richly emotional and argumentative forms but is aware of imaginative adventure.

'A Sign-Seeker', for example, beautifully articulates both a scientific piercing of veils and the thwarted energy of spiritual or spiritualist vision. (His illustration in *Wessex Poems* emblematizes this doubled seeking in drawing the stars and a huge comet in a dark sky.) The speaker spends nearly half the poem on completed apprehensions of the phenomenal world, in many tones, then slightly more than half the poem on noumenal imaginings. These are beautiful yearnings and dreams of personal survivals, like 'heart to heart returning after dust to dust' and they are also made political and ethical, when he sees 'Earth's Frail lie bleeding of her Strong' or desires 'one plume as pledge that Heaven inscrolls the wrong'. The story teems with images and incidents of imaginative scope, in order to mark efforts, limits and failures, starkly stated:

Such scope is granted not to lives like mine . . .
    I have lain in dead men's beds, have walked
    The tombs of those with whom I had talked,
Called many a gone and goodly one to shape a sign . . .

Domestic furniture and simple statement are poignant: that second line turns a then common occurrence into an uncommon image for desperate ghost-hunting, in which that sad echo of 'dead' in 'beds' plays its part. The last line of the poem is characteristically similar, blunt, curt and physical, following a conceptual and abstract personification. Speech is dead simple as it instances mortality: 'And Nescience mutely muses: When a man falls he lies.' The poem presses hard, but not tirelessly or endlessly, against limits.

In 'The House of Silence' Hardy images a pierced screen of matter, a metaphor and synecdoche for reaching through phenomenal to noumenal experience. But first we get another metaphor and synecdoche, in the house. A child and an adult stand outside, in an immediate rendering of threshold and imagining. The child is un-Wordsworthianly unimaginative, stubbornly stopping short at appearances and having to be told that the silent house is teeming with imaginative busyness. The solid walls through which nothing and nobody are visible become a screen of matter, penetrable by those who 'bear / The visioning powers of soul' and 'dare to pierce the material screen'. The appearance of the house is one of funereal enclosure but as dialogue moves on we move inside to find further thresholds, figures not visible to the child, 'funeral shades that seem / The uncanny scenery of a dream,' performing a festival of music, laughter and light for the spinning brain. This is the activity of the inhabitant's poetic vision, implied at the start of the poem and identified at the end. It is called visionary but it can imaginatively pass the boundaries of death and time to comprehend past and present, Heaven and Earth, and compress 'an aeon in an hour'. The thresholds observable to the average outside view are set up to praise creative scope. The poet's, not the philosopher's, imagination can pass between the material and the immaterial, as Hardy imagines his necessary angel, which respects agnosticism. Compounding image and story like 'Self Unseeing', the poem precisely imagines imagination, setting vision within vision.

Crossings from the natural to the supernatural experience are frequently made in Hardy's many playful and serious ghost poems, though some of his ghosts, however personal and personified in hauntings and survivals, appear or speak to assert a biological continuity. In 'Transformations', for instance, the dead are imagined 'not underground, / But as nerves and veins . . . / In the growths of upper air,' and in 'proud Songsters', Hardy startlingly and instructively contemplates not post-mortal but pre-mortal life, 'a year ago, or less than twain', when the finches, nightingales and thrushes were 'particles of grain, / And earth, and air, and rain'. James Richardson says, in *Thomas Hardy. The Poetry of Necessity*, that Hardy creates a 'magnificent spiritualism' showing 'that the past fights its way to its own energy, struggles back into human awareness, back into immortality', and though I would add that the spiritualism is entertained rather than accepted, and wryly asserts a lack of scope and inexorable limits, I find the word 'magnificent' sympathetic and appropriate for Hardy's pride and struggle, as he imagines.

Most of these attempts at such a complex emotional projection from living to dying and death, self to other, human to non-human nature, are brilliantly various. But his most famous attempts to imagine the dead, and imagine the dead conscious of the living, are at their most dramatically and experientially varied in the poems he wrote after his first wife's death in 1912. For Hardy, as for everyone, bereavement necessarily involved the sense of limits and barriers, in past and future, as well as the desire to cross or transcend them, or imagine doing so. The 1913 elegies and many later poems he went on writing about Emma are poems in which limit usually becomes unbearable. Just as his poetry of unbelief is never static but reflects and renews his longings, refusals, thwartings and ironies, in a continuum, so the lyrics of bereavement continue for the rest of his long writing life, renewing the experience of loss, remorse, restoration, rejection and desire.

In 'The Haunter' – to take one of many examples – he imagines death from the dead woman's viewpoint, invoking an intolerably tantalizing sense of barrier as he imagines return and close – actually measured – proximity. The ghost imagines him imagining her, but she is given a voice to say she is dumb. So the whole poem pushes against the limits of the inarticulate, most deeply reflexive about imaginative failure and success, but also most simply, and remorsefully, admitting the lack of communication in life:

> He does not think that I haunt here nightly:
>   How shall I let him know
> That whither his fancy sets him wandering
>   I, too, alertly go? –
> Hover and hover a few feet from him
>   Just as I used to do,
> But cannot answer the words he lifts me –
>   Only listen thereto!
>
> When I could answer he did not say them:
>   When I could let him know
> How I would like to join in his journeys
>   Seldom he wished to go.

One of the most heart-rending lines in Hardy's poetry is that 'Hover and hover a few feet from him' and what follows. Read in isolation those eight words with the repeated verb sound ghostlike, in position and motion. But the impression is weirdly tranformed into a memory of earthly habit, 'Just as I used to do', with all that it implies, presenting the ghostly image of hovering as a shocking metaphor for physical and emotional distance, neglect, and hesitancy in daily life.

Though the poem ends with a consolation, the ghost benevolently wishing to bring him peace and assuring him of goodwill and fidelity, the shifting imagery of limits sets up a strong undertow. The ghost's benison and posthumous forgiveness is desperately needed by the poet-widower, but it is a frailer presence in the poem, projected across the ghostly rift, than the recollection of the old rift between the living pair, and as a conclusion, after such a beginning, it makes wish-fulfilment transparent. The poem seems to tell a truth in spite of repression: perhaps once that hovering was imagined it was unconsciously translated into remembered distance. And the repeated words of closeness, 'Close as his shade' and 'Near as I reach', resound with deepened irony and remorse. The sense of threshold and limit is compounded and converted, to make a story of generous haunting into a ghost's reproach, tactful, muted, but clearly audible. The tug away from reproach at the end, suggesting an imagination too engrossed in itself, makes clear the listener's unwillingness to hear all the ghost would say. It is as if Emma Hardy had taken a hand in the poem, as a bitter ghost might, responding to invocation. Since imagination raises ghosts, and can be seized by them, she did. It was as risky for Hardy to invoke ghosts as for Lady Macbeth to raise up unsexing spirits. Poetry is ritual, and commits its performer to unconscious forces.

He perhaps realized that the poem which does for a human being – his dead wife – was what this poem does for the deer, because 'On Stinsford Hill at Midnight' is placed immediately before 'The Fallow Deer at the Lonely House' in *Late Lyrics and Earlier*. Hardy's placing gives the hint. Another ghost-poem about Emma Hardy's death, it imagines another creature's imaginative independence, which is to abjure imagining the other for the self. Though of course each elegy is separate and different, this one undermines or questions a number of the most famous and most romantic elegies reviving that ancient flame, which have been so simplified and – to my mind – misinterpreted by being considered in a mass (for instance, by Donald Davie and Tim Armstrong, who take opposite views).[2]

In 'The Monument-Maker' the woman's ghost rejected the memorial and challenges the elegist, but here she is further removed, unaware of the survivor and behaving

in ways he finds incomprehensible. He is haunted in a
bizarre and uncompanionable fashion, not at all in his
ghost's usual style, in a discomforting elegy. At first the
woman is not recognized as she is seen singing on the hill
and taking no notice of him. In a second glimpse he sees
that she is strumming a timbrel but he still cannot make
her out, puzzled both by her identity and by what she is
doing on 'the blank hill', and calling her antics 'strange'
and 'phantastry'. (She seems a little mad, as Hardy and his
biographers speculated that Emma was, but the ghost's
madness seems right for a ghost's new wild free state.)
Assuming that the ghost is there for him, and performing
for him, he questions her airiness – a great idea for ghostly
insouciance – and her placidity, but he has to make all
the running. He recognizes her abruptly in the fourth
stanza, 'Why such from you?', the poem concentrating
wonderfully on its ghost and leaving the reader to follow
its course, but is unnerved by her independence of feeling,
song and dance, and total neglect of him. Trying – most
imaginatively – to appropriate her through her happiness,
he begs her to come nearer, her note is just what he
needs. He envies, questions and perhaps laments:

> 'This world is dark, and where you are',
> I said, 'I cannot be,'
> But still the happy one sang on,
> And had no need of me.

It is perhaps Hardy's most original ghost poem, and a
highly original elegy. In it he sheds the assumption that
the dead woman's haunting is for him, imagines an
independence more daunting than antagonism, and allows
the ghost the space which he grants to the deer, the
insects and the thrush. Another example of Hardy's insuf-
iciently praised terseness, it is a short bare lyric which
crams into small compass the moral development of a

whole *Bildungsroman*. What the rejected narrator discovers
is what Gwendolen Harleth discovers in *Daniel Deronda*
and Gabriel Conroy in 'The Dead', another's independent
existence outside the possessive imagination. Hardy's
haunted man thinks he can cross the threshold from life
to death, and from past to present, which he imagined, or
almost imagined, in some of the elegies, but instead he
finds and crosses a real threshold, of possessive appropriation. The discovery activates the empathetic imagination,
negative capability. Unlike George Eliot's and Joyce's
gravely disturbed moral adventurers, Hardy's tells the story
of imagination modestly and unassumingly.

RETICENCE

Imaginative limit is subject and form. In 'The Haunter'
and other elegies, the reader is offered an ironic subtext
or deconstruction which is existentially and morally
instructive and in 'On Stinsford Hill' a more direct
acknowledgement. The combination of reserve and suggestiveness stamps many of Hardy's spare and understated
poems. He is drawn to a combination of narrative and
lyric, and several of his poems depend on a gap in the
narrative which preserves, but also threatens the threshold
between the isolated intensity of lyric and the fullness or
continuity of narrative. The reserve or subtext may seem
like the result of an unwilled resistance to a willed
conclusion, but it can often seem a simple effect of control
and restraint, a grim or melancholy teasing that fits a
mourning mood and the poet's moody inclination.

In 'Castle Boterel' for instance, the implicit love story,
hinted at, not told, creates a gap in order to give the
highest value to the experience, in Hardy's favourite
occupatio. The poem refuses to say what the lovers did and
said as they climbed but there is the unmistakable praise,
'But was there ever / A time of such quality, since or

before, / In that hill's story?' In spite of the wary admission of subjectivity, 'To one mind never', the declaration is one of the most powerful utterances of love in Hardy's love poetry. The poem offers a simple model of suggestiveness, a pregnant moment in art, as Lessing called the sculptor's achievement of incompletion and momentariness, which aptly forms words for a pregnant moment in life, 'It filled but a minute'. The poem gives that sense of teeming overflow with which this often dour poet can astonish us, like his wintry old thrush. It articulates the ineffable and also, less grandly, dodges the difficulty of finding an objective correlative for joy.

As I have said, brief but condensed expressive understatement makes style and structure in 'After a Romantic Day' where the lack of romantic landscape, beyond a minimal moonlight, is welcome to the heart and mind of a character brooding on the day's experience, and created for him by the reticent and sentimentally sophisticated poet wanting to concentrate on feeling not narrative:

> And the blank lack of any charm
>   Of landscape did no harm.
> The bald steep cutting, rigid, rough,
>   And moon-lit, was enough
> For poetry of place: its weathered face
> Formed a convenient sheet whereon
> The visions of his mind were drawn.

We are presented simply with what the poet wants us to feel – remembered bliss, but no narrative detail. The objective correlative, or its absence, in the bald cutting, is like the bareness of the narrative. Both at first sight represent denial. The man-made cutting looks unpromisingly destructive, but it shows a mineral surface, and though unattractive in itself, is not unpleasant, because its lack of beauty and individuality do not interfere with reverie. Similarly, the poet's withdrawal of narrative detail sets our reverie in motion.

Romance vibrates in a similar absence, emphasized by a stanzaic gap, in the magical 'When I Set out for Lyonnesse'. This is another ambitiously short poem about experience too intimate for disclosure. Hugging its reverie to itself, it tells us even less than 'After a Romantic Day'. In the first stanza the speaker looks ahead in fantasy and expectation, but denies forecast: 'No prophet durst declare'. In the second he looks back at the past, 'When I came back. . . ./ All marked with mute surmise / My radiance rare and fathomless'. He leaves out what happened in between going and returning, in Lyonnesse. The place name, which he sometimes uses for Wessex but here for the west Cornish coast, and the metaphors of wizardry and magic, have associations with Arthur's drowned city, and hint at the nature of the unexplained experience. A barrier is teasingly set up, first within the poem, and then between the poem and reader, dividing the mute surmise and the fathomless radiance. For more than one reason, imaginative surmise is best left mute and the look of bliss may well be fathomless. The poem's reticence lets it stay so. We are left to surmise, and the adventure, like legendary drowned Lyonnesse, remains unfathomed. What vibrates across that threshold between wondering onlooker and secretive traveller, is equivocal. This poem utters an intense delight, showing that Hardy's expressive reticence adapts itself to the later troubled passions and purposes rather than originating in troubles that needed repression, secrecy or consolation.

Such silence is the subject of many poems about limits or barriers, where characters do not communicate, or where they do not see or understand every aspect of an experience or a time or a place, as in 'Overlooking the River Stour'. Here we begin with three stanzas of incisive visualization, imaging low-flying swallows, moorhens, and closed kingcups in the rain, phenomena whose appearances and motion are closely observed by the person looking out of a window. Observation is suggested by the sharp visual similes, unusual enough to be called conceits, which have the further function, along with the repetitions, of suggesting that theirs is an excessive imprint. This is confirmed in the last stanza in which visualization is dismissed as a displacement, but if we expect a complete explanation, we are disappointed:

> And never I turned my head, alack,
>   While these things met my gaze
>   Through the pane's drop-drenched glaze,
> To see the more behind my back. . . .
> O never I turned, but let, alack,
>   These less things hold my gaze!

The reader is presented only with the judgement. Having been made to concentrate like the speaker, on the incised scene outside the window, she is confronted by an absence of specification, and is in exactly the same position as the speaker has been, though without his knowledge. It is a poem which seems to offer conclusion, but denies access. The denial is not just a tease, because it gives the reader an experience of exclusion.

'The Division' begins with lovers apparently separated by bad weather and space:

> Rain on the windows, creaking doors,
>   With blasts that besom the green,
> And I am here, and you are there,
>   And a hundred miles between!

But the second verse begins 'O were it but the weather, Dear', and explains that they are actually separated by something else. We may expect the riddle to be solved in the third verse, as it is in a way, but incompletely and teasingly because the division turns out to be something that cannot be named, presented in a topos of horrified inexpressibility, as 'that thwart thing' . . . 'which nothing cleaves or clears'. Of course it has been speculatively identified by biographers, like the experience overlooked in 'Overlooking the River Stour', but the poem deliberately refrains from identifying it. The answer is left to the imagination, which is frustrated, encouraged, then made to take no for an answer, left divided, as the people in the poem are, but from the explanation.

It is not that biographers are wrong to change the poem, since a resolute and sensitive reader can wrest it back from them, but it seems a pity not to praise such powerful reticence. Hardy may have left out – as I am doing now – certain specificities of experience because he thought them shocking or scandalous or likely to cause pain, but the omission makes for a special kind of poem, which originates in a specific event but chooses to omit, gaining a general application and the sense of privacy. When Hardy wants to be specfic, then he is, clearly. In some of the elegies, for example, he makes no bones about admitting that the relationship which was bound to be identified as his marriage had been unhappy.

When Hardy writes about crossing or failing to cross boundaries that challenge or frustrate his characters, he often constructs thresholds which the reader may want to cross or fail to cross. One of these poems, 'In her Precincts' uses that favourite Victorian image of the window, which here works complexly. A lover shut out in the cold and dark first interprets the darkness of his beloved's windows as sympathetically cold, inactive and gloomy:

> And the square of each window a dull black blur
>   Where showed no stir:

Yes, her gloom within at the lack of me
Seemed matching mine at the lack of her.

But 'As the eveshade swathed the house and lawn' and
the lights go on he realizes that it is not gloom but 'glee
within' and the windows change signification, imaging
'severance' for himself alone. What might be a threshold,
the outside of the house, is seen as a limit. A space
between two stanzas acts as a crossing-point and a barrier
to entry and imaginative construction. The teller makes
his imaginative essay but his imagination has to be corrected. Hardy enjoys exploiting the structural divisions
and pauses of stanzaic form, and the formality, which has
sometimes been judged arbitrary and mechanical, has
often the function of exaggerating and emphasizing such
thresholds and temporary stops.

In 'Before and After Summer' a pause in the poem
once again acts as a structural symbol. This space between
stanzas is an apparent bridge but a large gap, formally
marked by the numbering:

I

Looking forward to the spring
One puts up with anything.
On this February day
Though the winds leap down the street,
Wintry scourgings seem but play,
And these later shafts of sleet
– Sharper pointed than the first –
And these later snows – the worst –
Are as a half-transparent blind
Riddled by rays from sun behind.

II

Shadows of the October pine
Reach into this room of mine:

On the pine there swings a bird;
He is shadowed with the tree.
Mutely perched he bills no word;
Blank as I am even is he.
For those happy suns are past,
Fore-discerned in winter last.
When went by their pleasure, then?
I, alas, perceived not when.

That eloquent gap between the stanza contains the
passage of spring and summer, all the months between
sharp February and shadowed October. It also contains
the heart of the poem. The thresholds of time are cruelly
marked as the speaker first ignores the present in February
anticipation of spring and sun, and looks back at the
happy summer whose passing he never noticed, the suns
he missed or mis-imagined. He saw them, indirectly,
through his winter anticipation, compounding the gap and
the missed moment. Autumn is recorded not in the classical
symbolism of fall and decay, but reticently, through a
natural absence of the bird's seasonal spring-and-summer
song which is metaphorically grazed by the literal but
suggestive 'mutely' and 'blank'. As so often Hardy relies on
expressive construction, and keeps his language quiet and
understated. The 'alas' makes its presence felt the more
weightily after the light touch of that autumn image. The
simple, enigmatic, poem registers a moving failure to
catch and keep the present moment and its momentary
happiness. It also makes a complex memory of anticipa-
tory hope, enacting time limits for the poet and narrative
limits for the reader. The absence in the centre, between
the stanzas, creates the energy and frustration of an act of
imagination, an act which summons a deep melancholy
for an untold story. The blank silence in the poem,
doubled by the mute bird, stands also for the silence of
the poem, and the blankness of its story, performing the

same function as the bare railway cutting in 'After a Romantic Day'. Its subject reminds me of Henry James's superficially very different story of missed experience, 'The Beast in the Jungle'. Hardy's short reticent poem is more mysterious and more muted. Its story, like James's, is that there is no story, but although James masters gaps and absences when he wants to, in his story we are told precisely what his unheroic hero missed. In Hardy's poem, we miss it too, though we feel its aftermath. We are made to concentrate not on the morality of passive living and hyperactive imagination, but on the contrast between a strong desire and nothing.

It is an extreme example, but Hardy is a great storyteller who often needs and likes to negate narrative specificity, to create an absence of characters and actions. Reading such poems, we are like Hardy respecting the night-insects or listening to the old thrush or wanting to hug to himself what happened on the romantic day or not daring to utter what the thwart thing was. We understand the poet's language, and something of his feelings, but it is used to preserve its heart-secrets and life-mysteries. He loves a good long story, but some stories he wants to guard, and some he may not wholly understand. We are confronted with an emotional utterance but denied completion, causality or objective correlative. Like Hardy feeling for the natural world from the human side of a boundary between the self and the others, we release, or have released for us, an outgoing sympathy or empathy, recognizing the limits of knowledge and imagination, by trial, error, inhibition and respect. Hardy keeps his secrets as he makes his reduced and unromantic claims for the imagination's access to truth and wholeness.

Such omissions, reductions, invitations and displacements are congenial to modern readers practised in the appreciation of openness, fracture, displacement, deconstruction and lisibility, who are educated to be wary of wholeness, harmony, completeness and closure. Hardy reminds us that pre-modern writers, despite partisan and jealous critical fictions about their essentialism and idealism, may be more at home with uncertainty and hesitation than we expect, can pause before the apparently noumenal, visionary and essential, or leave out the specification, to admit, identify, check and destabilize imagination's tendency to idealize, systematize, blend and unify. Hardy uses his poetry in ways that require the reader to experience checks, halts, gaps, limited access and impassable thresholds, and question the conventions of completion.

Such narrative reticence is common in lyric, part of its generic conditions. We occasionally experience something comparable in the novels. For instance, in the early novel *A Pair of Blue Eyes* there is the large gap in Elfride's experience, after her engagement with Knight is broken off. Her marriage, illness and death fill this gap, and when they are discovered by her two old lovers on her funeral train, their shock, like their ignorance, is shared by the reader. Hardy may have contrived it as a melodramatic winding-up, but for a modern reader, it has come to seem an eloquent gap and shock, politically tragic, compounding the marginalizing of a woman's domestic existence, and death, in a busy professional and conventional man's world.

Such gaps and absences are very rare in Hardy's novels, innovative in many ways but generally bounded by the Victorian fictions of completion. However, elisions and lacunae are easily accommodated, and often demanded, in lyric poetry, and Hardy occasionally extends the advantage of lyric to his dramatic monologues and ballads, several of which have enigmatically compressed plots and half-open or suggestive endings. This structural play is writerly, demanding and exciting the reader's participation.

Notes

CHAPTER ONE: PORTRAITS OF THE ARTIST IN THE NOVELS

1 This poem is discussed by Joan Grundy in *Thomas Hardy and the Sister Arts*, a book dealing with Hardy's assimilation and knowledge of other arts, and with his self-awareness, to which this study is in a way complementary.

2 He can look at lightning without blinking, which Jean Brooks in *Thomas Hardy: the Poetic Structure* says is a mark of the devil.

3 I have discussed Jude's Virgilian but more Horatian vision in the next chapter.

4 Geoffrey Grigson, editing the novel for the New Wessex Edition, asserts in the introduction and notes that the novel's, and the last chapter's, title is not taken from Shakespeare but from a sixteenth- or seventeenth-century ballad of that title which Hardy would have known from William Chappell's *Popular Music of the Olden Time* (1859). This is nonsense: if Hardy knew the ballad 'describing rustic merrymaking under the woodland tree', it would not have erased but reinforced Shakespeare, who dramatized rustic as well as aristocratic merrymaking under the greenwood tree, as well as much else relevant to the novel. Some Shakespearean resonances may not have been spotted because they are subtle, but that does not apply to the wonderful bird–human 'Come hithers', which are not annotated.

5 In his introduction to the New Wessex edition.

6 *The Life and Work of Thomas Hardy*, ed. Millgate.

CHAPTER TWO: CENTRES OF CREATIVITY IN THE NOVELS: FROM GABRIEL TO TESS

1 Kenneth Marsden demurs a little at my treatment of 'bullheaded' Henchard in this chapter, and interprets the last will and testament

as characteristic defiance. He may be right: the bloodyminded Henchard is clearly the least reflective of the creative characters and I may be inclined to elevate him, but he has imagination even if he does not always use it and I would not leave him out.

2 The auto-didacticism is only relative, since Hardy was educated until he was sixteen, then continued to study while working as an architect.

3 Her capacity to imagine is historical, metaphysical, and even meta-fictional, since she determines the novel's ending, suggesting to Angel that he marry Liza-Lu, taking a hand in the tragic plot and Shakespeareanly imagining an extra or alternative ending. Know-ledgeably, sensibly, and anti-clerically, she anticipates and sweeps aside the church's objection to marrying a deceased wife's sister. The ingenious error-spotter John Sutherland does not notice this, and he is in error to suggest that Hardy omits to mention the forbidden degrees. ('Who will Angel marry next?', *Can Jane Eyre Be Happy?*) It is not the kind of mistake the well-informed agnostic Hardy would make.

CHAPTER THREE: GOOD TIMES IN *JUDE THE OBSCURE*: CONSTRUCTING FICTIONS

1 Reprinted in Roger Gard's *Henry James. The Critical Muse: Selected Literary Criticism.*

2 Terry Eagleton and Patricia Ingham, in their respective introduc-tions to New Wessex and World's Classics editions of *Jude.*

3 In Virgil's *Aeneid*, Book I, Aeneas sees his mother Venus by the sea, youthful and radiant, skirts kilted for hunting, emerging from 'the heart of the woodland' to confirm his Roman mission.

4 'Art as Technique' (1917) reprinted in *Russian Formalist Criticism: Four Essays.*

5 I have corrected one apparent slip in the punctuation of this passage in the New Wessex edition.

CHAPTER FOUR: PORTRAITS OF THE ARTIST IN THE POEMS

1 But it is dangerous to generalize about Hardy's allusions, which are a subject in themselves. Some may be invisible scaffolding useful to

the artist but not necessary to the reader, like some of the elaborate classical allusions proposed by Paul Turner in *The Life of Thomas Hardy* – for instance, the Virgilian references in *Desperate Remedies*, which are obviously present but when recognized do not enlarge or enhance or change our response to the novel. Some allusion goes deep, like the echoes of *As You Like It* in *Under the Greenwood Tree* (see my Chapter One) or of *King Lear* in *The Return of the Native*.

Scholars tend to argue that their finds are complex revelations, but allusion may be more personally expressive than structurally or thematically purposive. Some may be pedantic and redundant allusions originating in Hardy's love of learned reference. A more complicated example is the extensive use of Tennyson in *A Pair of Blue Eyes*: there are Tennysonian allusions in epigraphs and text, including seven quotations, five from *In Memoriam*. (When Hardy met Tennyson in 1880 he was pleased by the poet's praise of the novel.) It was published in 1873, shortly after Hardy's friend Horace Moule committed suicide, and as the character of Henry Knight resembles Moule, and Hardy quotes from the elegy in which Tennyson imagines his dead friend Hallam's imagination, the Tennysonian references, which sit loosely in their context, may be unconscious tributes to his friend and mentor, proleptic memorials. I have discussed these references in *Tennyson and the Novelists*, published as a Tennyson Society Occasional Paper, No. 9, 1993.

CHAPTER FIVE: ARTS OF CONVERSATION

1 In Dylan Thomas's conversation poem 'If my head hurt a hair's foot' a woman (imagined by the poet who is a man) answers the unborn ungendered child in a similar solicitous love which knows it lacks power. Compared with other poems which imagine on behalf of a child, for instance, Yeats's 'Prayer for my Daughter' or Seamus Heaney's 'Act of Union', Hardy's and Thomas's are unauthoritarian and unegocentric, imaginatively refusing to imagine for another creature.

CHAPTER SIX: THE POETRY OF PLACE

1 Marsden has an interesting discussion of this phrase in *The Poetry of Thomas Hardy*.

2 Davie, *Thomas Hardy and British Poetry*.

3 Tim Armstrong in his Introduction to *Thomas Hardy. Selected Poems* disagrees (as I do) with Davie's belief that Emma is 'an absolute presence in the landscape of memory' and that the end of 'After a Journey' has 'an unprecedented serenity', and says 'it seems' to him (I think on slight grounds) that the declaration at the end 'can only be read ironically and hopelessly'.

4 One of Shakespeare's structural trademarks is the request for narrative recapitulation at the end of the plays, for instance in Hamlet's and Othello's injunctions, or in the comedies and romances where the characters ask to hear the whole story in which they have played a part, so know only in part. (I have discussed this in *Shakespeare's Storytellers*.) Like Shakespeare from whom he and George Eliot, in *Silas Marner*, may have got the idea which they both simplify, Hardy creates an oscillating conclusion. He closes the novel by suggesting that Clym's story is known, opens it to make the characters seem real, with a future, opens it to generate more story, and closes it to admit fictionality.

CHAPTER SEVEN: SEXUAL IMAGINATION: THE MONOLOGUES

1 Unlike Thackeray and George Eliot, Hardy does not attribute gender to his chief narrators in the novels.

2 Marsden draws attention to this (*op. cit.*).

3 Hynes, vol II, p. 516.

CHAPTER EIGHT: THRESHOLDS AND LIMITS

1 See Note 3 to Chapter Six.

2 The best discussion of this subject is in Hynes, *The Pattern of Hardy's Poetry*.

Select Booklist

1 HARDY'S WORKS

The Novels of Thomas Hardy, New Wessex Edition, London: Macmillan, 1974–5. All quotations of the novels are from this edition.

The Complete Poetical Works of Thomas Hardy, vols 1–3, ed. Samuel Hynes, Oxford: Clarendon Press, 1982–5. All quotations of the poems are from this edition.

The Life and Work of Thomas Hardy, Thomas Hardy, ed. Michael Millgate, London: Macmillan, 1984.

2 CRITICISM AND BIOGRAPHY

Armstrong, Tim, *Thomas Hardy. Selected Poems*, London: Longman, 1993.

Davie, Donald, *Thomas Hardy and British Poetry*, London: Routledge & Kegan Paul, 1973.

Gittings, Robert, *The Young Thomas Hardy*, London: Heinemann, 1975.

Grundy, Joan, *Hardy and the Sister Arts*, London: Macmillan, 1972.

Hynes, Samuel, *The Pattern of Hardy's Poetry*, Chapel Hill: University of North Carolina Press, 1961.

James, Henry, *The Critical Muse: Selected Literary Criticism*, ed. Roger Gard, Harmondsworth: Penguin, 1987.

Marsden, Kenneth, *The Poems of Thomas Hardy: A Critical Introduction*, London: Athlone Press, 1969.

Millgate, Michael, *Thomas Hardy: a Biography*, Oxford: Oxford University Press, 1982.

Richardson, James, *Thomas Hardy: The Poetry of Necessity*, Chicago and London: University of Chicago Press, 1975, 1977.

Shklovsky, Victor, 'Art as Technique' (1917) reprinted in *Russian Formalist Criticism: Four Essays*, ed. Lee T. Lemon and Marion J. Reis, Lincoln: University of Nebraska Press, 1965.

Sutherland, John, *Can Jane Eyre Be Happy?*, Oxford: World's Classics, 1997.

Index

Anon., 134–5
Arnold, Matthew, 121, 179
Armstrong, Tim, 207, 221
Austen, Jane, 2, 59, 75, 106–8

Bakhtin, Mikhail, 75
Barnes, William, 172
Barthélémon, François Hippolyte, 86
Baudelaire, Charles, 174
Beckett, Samuel, 57, 121
Book of Common Prayer, 48–9
Brontë, Charlotte, 47, 58, 106
Brontë, Emily, 152–3
Brooke, Rupert, 158
Brooks, Jean, 218
Browning, Robert, 163, 174
Bunyan, John, 52, 60

Carroll, Lewis, 39, 173
Cervantes, Miguel de, 59
Chappell, William, 218
Clough, Arthur Hugh, 161
Cockerell, Sydney, 175–6
Coleridge, Samuel Taylor, 16, 45, 47, 73, 93, 102, 114, 120, 135, 138, 143, 153, 166, 186
Compton Burnett, 1, 21, 106–7
Congreve, William, 106
Coward, Noel, 106

Davie, Donald, 142, 207, 221
De Bono, Edward, 90
Defoe, Daniel, 58

Dickens, Charles, 1, 16, 29, 31, 41, 47, 67, 119, 136
Donne, John, 179

Eagleton, Terry, 64, 219
Eliot, George, 1, 2, 12, 16, 21, 33, 38, 41, 47, 60, 75, 106, 112, 177, 179, 200, 209, 221
Eliot, T.S, 21
Ellis, Havelock, 13–14
Empson, William, 173

Fitzgerald, F. Scott, 75
Freud, Sigmund, 120
Fontane, Theodor de, 57, 75

Gittings, Robert, 9
Goethe, Johann Wolfgang von, 1, 39
Grigson, Geoffrey, 22, 218
Grundy, Joan, 218

Hardy, Emma, née Gifford, 143–150, 205–9, 213
Hardy, Florence, née Dugdale, 140, 149, 160
Hardy, Mary, née Head, 23, 151–2
Harper's New Monthly Magazine, 61, 63, 79
Hazlitt, William, 184
Heaney, Seamus, 220
Herbert, George, 94, 179, 202
Herrick, Robert, 185
Holme, Constance, 107

Homer, 3, 154, 167
Hopkins, Gerard Manley, 86, 186
Horace, 64–66, 72, 185
Housman, A.E., 147
Hughes, Ted, 195, 198
Huxley, Aldous, 106
Hynes, Samuel, 221

Ingham, Patricia, 64, 219

James, Henry, 1, 2, 47, 60, 61, 75, 106, 167, 168, 179, 216
Joyce, James, 1, 15, 17, 33, 45, 46, 64, 65, 86, 154, 209

Kafka, Franz, 39, 141
Kavanagh, Patrick, 64
Keats, John, 10, 33, 86–88, 135, 138, 184, 200
Ken, Thomas (Bishop), 86
Koestler, Arthur, 115

Lawrence, D.H., 14, 25, 44, 45, 49, 149, 152, 179, 185
Lessing, Gotthold E, 210

Macneice, Louis, 75, 202
Mann, Thomas, 16
Marlowe, Christoper, 39, 176
Marsden, Kenneth, 218–9, 221
Meredith, George, 85–86
Mill, John Stuart, 81, 164
Milton, John, 92
Moule, Horace, 220
Mozart, Amadeus von, 86

Owen, Wilfred, 158

Peacock, Thomas Love, 106
Pinter, Harold, 106

Pope, Alexander, 1
Proust, Marcel, 15, 16, 33, 187, 193
Psalms, 69
Richardson, James, 205
Richardson, Samuel, 16

Shakespeare, William, 8, 21, 22, 24, 29, 31, 33, 40, 41, 42, 54, 76, 85, 89, 119, 135, 143, 155–6, 158, 174, 207, 218, 219, 220, 221
Shaw, Bernard, 163
Shelley, Percy Bysshe, 85, 87–89, 196–8
Shklovsky, Victor, 73
Sophocles, 167
Spenser, Edmund, 79
Stendhal, 74, 162
Stevenson, Robert Louis, 183
Sutherland, John, 219
Swinburne, Algernon, 86, 161

Tennyson, Alfred, Lord, 7, 85, 148, 196, 220
Thackeray, William Makepeace, 1, 16, 47, 75, 77, 221
Thomas, Dylan, 220
Tolstoy, Leo, 112
Turner, Paul, 22, 220

Verlaine, Paul, 1
Virgil, 15, 65, 219, 220

Wagner, Richard, 8
Westminster Review, The, 13–14
Wilde, Oscar, 106–7, 174, 183
Woolf, Virginia, 12, 65
Wordsworth, William, 11, 64, 102, 135, 151–2, 153, 186, 187, 204

Yeats, William Butler, 65, 93, 149